Essay Index

Essays IN
APPRECIATION

BOOKS BY JOHN LIVINGSTON LOWES

CONVENTION AND REVOLT IN POETRY
THE ROAD TO XANADU
OF READING BOOKS
GEOFFREY CHAUCER
ESSAYS IN APPRECIATION

Essays IN APPRECIATION

John Livingston Lowes

KENNIKAT PRESS, INC./PORT WASHINGTON, N. Y.

Essay Index

FOR
M. C. L.

Acknowledgments

THE kind permission of the British Academy, through its President, to reprint 'The Art of Geoffrey Chaucer,' and of *The Yale Review* to reprint the copyrighted essay, 'Two Readings of Earth,' is gratefully acknowledged. And similar thanks are due to the *Harvard Alumni Bulletin*, the *Saturday Review of Literature*, and *The Nation* for their courtesy in the case, respectively, of 'The Noblest Monument of English Prose,' 'The Poetry of Amy Lowell,' and 'An Unacknowledged Imagist.'

J. L. L.

Contents

The Noblest Monument of
English Prose

The Noblest Monument of English Prose

I HAVE deliberately refrained from naming in my title the masterpiece to which my descriptive phrase applies, because I wish to leave no question of the one and only aspect of a rich and complex subject which I mean to treat. For the monument of English prose to be considered is the King James version of the Bible. Of its unique significance in the field of English letters there can be no doubt. Its phraseology has become part and parcel of our common tongue — bone of its bone and flesh of its flesh. Its rhythms and cadences, its turns of speech, its familiar imagery, its very words, are woven into the texture of our literature, prose and poetry alike. Yet it is of the Orient, we of the West; it is a translation, not an original; and it has reached us by way, not of one language only, but of three. What is it, then, in this translation, which has made it a factor of such power in the development of our speech? What are the qualities which have stamped indelibly its very phraseology upon the literary masterpieces of 300 years? What, in particular, is the nature of the long evolution through which the noble

3

vehicle of a great and deeply significant literature clothed itself at last in English words? Those, and those alone, are the questions which I shall try in part to answer.

Consider for a moment (to deal with the obvious first) our own familiar, everyday speech — the apt and telling turns of expression, the phrases of homely vigour or happy pregnancy which have become a part of our linguistic stock in trade. 'Highways and hedges,' 'hip and thigh,' 'arose as one man,' 'lick the dust,' 'a thorn in the flesh,' 'a broken reed,' 'the root of all evil,' 'the nether millstone,' 'the sweat of his brow,' 'heap coals of fire,' 'a soft answer,' 'a word in season,' 'weighed and found wanting,' 'we are the people' — that is a list of Biblical phrases cited in a recent volume, and most of us could double it or treble it at will. The English of the Bible has a pithiness and raciness, a homely tang, a terse sententiousness, an idiomatic flavour which comes home to men's business and bosoms. And among the qualities which a saturation in the Bible has always lent to English style is a happiness of incidental phrase and a swift tellingness of diction which only a similar saturation in Shakespeare can approach in its effectiveness.

But the influence of the English of the Bible is deeper and more pervasive far than that. And it is another aspect of this influence of which I wish particularly to speak. For the Biblical style is characterized not merely by homely vigour and pithiness of phrase, but also by a singular nobility

4

of diction and by a rhythmic quality which is, I think, unrivalled in its beauty. And I know no better way of reaching an understanding of the unique position which the King James version of the Bible occupies as a monument of prose than an attempt to reach the secret of its diction and its rhythms. And that, with no pretence of completeness, is what I mean to do.

I

It is not too much to say, I think, that the language of the English Bible owes its distinctive qualities, and that perhaps in no unequal measure, on the one hand to the vast desert spaces and wide skies of the hither Orient, and on the other to the open seas and rock-bound coasts of England. Nor do I mean that in the least as a mere figure of speech. For at the beginning of the long chain of development which makes the very language of the English Bible what it is are the men who, beside the rivers of Babylon and Egypt, or among the hills and pasture lands of Israel and Judah, or in the wide stillness of Arabia, brooded and wondered and dreamed, and left a language simple and sensuous and steeped in the picturesque imagery of what they saw and felt. At the end of this same chain of causes are the theatres of Shakespeare's London and the ships of the Elizabethan voyagers — of men whose language was as virile and as vivid as their lives. And between are the seventy at Alexandria and Jerome in his desert — Greece and Rome be-

tween Mesopotamia and England. How did the
elements fuse?

Once more let me repeat, we are concerned with
a *translation*. Now there are certain things which
are notoriously untranslatable.

> Not poppy nor mandragora,
> Nor all the drowsy syrups of the world
> Shall ever medicine thee to that sweet sleep
> Which thou ow'dest yesterday.

Some of you will recall a striking passage in which
Dr. Furness takes those lines and points out, word by
word, the utter impossibility of reproducing their
distinctive music or their subtle connotations in any
other language without irreparable loss. The very
essence of a piece of literature — its breath and finer
spirit — is apt to evaporate in the passage from one
language to another, so intimate is the union between the nicer shades of thought and feeling and
the delicate, evanescent associations of words. But
now we reach the first element in our analysis. For
Hebrew was a supremely translatable tongue, and
it was so, in large degree, because of certain qualities
of its vocabulary, which concern us closely here.

I spoke a moment ago — borrowing the words
from Milton's famous phrase about poetry — of the
Hebrew vocabulary as 'simple and sensuous.' Let
me be a little more explicit, and turn first to English for what my pedagogical friends would call
an 'apperceptive basis.' Everybody knows that
most of the words we use today to express intellectual, emotional, spiritual concepts had originally

physical significance. 'Wrong,' for example, primarily implied something twisted; 'implied' itself involves the idea of something folded within another thing — as 'involve' (to use what chance supplies!) rests on the concept of something rolled or wrapped about. 'Concept' itself, so considered, goes back to the notion of seizing or grasping; to 'consider,' in turn, was at first to gaze attentively upon the stars; 'attentively,' again, rests ultimately upon the idea of physical stretching — and so one might go on *ad libitum*. But with us these vivid physical implications of the words we use have all become attenuated, they have faded out. We no longer are conscious of their primitive, more concrete meaning; we should be not a little checked and disconcerted in our thinking if we were. In Hebrew, on the other hand, the vocabulary was consciously pictorial and concrete in its character. That which distinguishes the Semitic languages from the Aryan, says Renan, is the fact that 'this primitive union of sensation and idea persists — so that in each word one still hears the echo of the primitive sensations which determined the choice of the first makers of the language.' The writers of the Old Testament — and to a less degree those of the New as well — thought and felt and spoke in images — in a vocabulary compact of nearly all the physical sensations that flesh is heir to. 'Paul's words,' said Luther, 'are alive; they have hands and feet; if you cut them they bleed.' He might have said that with no less fitness of the Hebrew words.

Now this characteristic of the Hebrew vocabulary carries certain consequences which are pertinent to this discussion. In the first place, it gave to the diction of Hebrew literature an incomparable vividness. There is a famous passage in *Diana of the Crossways* in which Meredith speaks of the art of description: 'The art of the pen,' he says, 'is to rouse the inward vision, instead of labouring with a Drop-scene brush, as if it were to the eye; because our flying minds cannot contain a protracted description. That is why the poets, *who spring imagination with a word or phrase*, paint lasting pictures.' Well, to a degree unapproached, perhaps, unless it be in Shakespeare or in Dante, the Hebrew writers 'spring imagination with a word or phrase.' Their very words carry out Browning's curt injunction: 'do the thing shall breed the thought.' Instead of merely naming an emotion, they reproduce the physical sensation that attends it — the surging of blood to the face, the tingling of the nerves, the rising of the hair, the palsy of the tongue, the quickening of the breath.

> 'O God, thou art my God ... *my soul thirsteth* for thee, *my flesh longeth* for thee, in a dry and thirsty land where no water is'; 'As the hart panteth after the water brooks, so *panteth* my soul after thee'; 'Yet a little sleep, a little slumber, a little *folding of the hands* to sleep'; 'As the door *turneth upon his hinges*, so doth the slothful upon his bed'; 'Thou makest us a byword among the heathen, *a shaking of the head* among the people'; 'We walk in darkness, *we grope for the wall* like the blind'; 'I am weary of my crying: *my throat is dried: mine eyes fail* while I wait for my God.'

It would be easy to read such passages endlessly; these are enough to show to what degree the Biblical vocabulary is compact of the primal stuff of our common humanity — of its universal emotional, sensory experiences. The meaning of the Hebrew words is 'carried' — in Wordsworth's phrase — 'alive into the heart.'

Moreover, this same simple and sensuous quality shows itself in another way — in the inexpugnable racial tendency of the Hebrew mind to express not only emotions, but ideas, in apt and telling imagery. Poet and prophet and chronicler alike thought as well as felt in terms of what they had heard, what they had seen with their eyes, what they had looked upon and their hands handled. The large and simple and permanent objects and elements of life — the eternal hills, the treasures of the snow, rain coming down upon mown grass, winds and all weathers, the rock in the desert, still waters in pasture lands and the sea that roars and is troubled, sleep and the fleetingness of dreams — all the perennial, elemental processes of nature, all the changing yet abiding physiognomy of earth and sky were charged to their brooding eye with spiritual significance, and woven into the very texture of their speech.

> 'And a man shall be as an hiding place from the wind, and a covert from the tempest; as rivers of water in a dry place, as the shadow of a great rock in a weary land'; 'Thy righteousness is like the mountains of God; thy judgments are a great deep'; 'He

shall come down like rain upon the mown grass; as showers that water the earth'; 'Thou carriest them away as with a flood; they are as a sleep'; 'As a dream when one awaketh; so, O Lord, when thou awakest, thou shalt despise their image'; 'Surely I have stilled and quieted my soul; like a weaned child with his mother, my soul is with me like a weaned child'; 'Who shut up the sea with doors, when it brake forth, as if it had issued out of the womb? When I made the cloud the garment thereof, and thick darkness a swaddlingband for it'; 'Hast thou given the horse strength? hast thou clothed his neck with thunder?' 'As for man, his days are as grass: as a flower of the field, so he flourisheth. For the wind passeth over it, and it is gone; and the place thereof shall know it no more.'

Utter simplicity, limpid clearness, the vividness of direct, authentic vision — these are the salient qualities of the diction of the men who wrote the Bible.

Now let me return to what was said a few moments ago. The Hebrew of the Old Testament (and to a less degree the Greek of the New) is supremely translatable, and it is so largely because of just these salient characteristics of its diction — its simplicity, its clarity, its directness, and its universal and immediate appeal. And that brings us to another aspect of the subject. For it is the translation into English with which we have to do. And as regards possession of these same qualities, the English vocabulary, as it happens, can meet the Hebrew upon equal terms.

There are in the English vocabulary, as everybody knows, two chief elements — the one native, the other complexly foreign. And it is the fusion of these two which constitutes the unrivalled flexibility and variety of our speech. To its native, Saxon element it owes a homely vigour, a forthrightness and vividness and concreteness, an emotional appeal, in which it matches the Hebrew itself. To its foreign element — chiefly the Latin component, which will concern us in a moment — is due, among other things, a sonorousness, a stateliness, a richness of music, a capacity for delicate discrimination which makes it an instrument of almost endlessly varied stops. Now one element is predominant, now the other; more frequently there is an intimate fusion of the two. Every page of English literature, whether prose or poetry, illustrates the possibilities of infinite variety inherent in this fundamental character of English diction; but it is its bearing on the translation of the Bible which concerns us now, and to that I pass at once.

For reasons too complex and far-reaching for discussion here, the language at the period during which the Bible was being translated into English was in its most plastic stage. It was a time of intense living, of incomparable zest in life. England was literally, in Milton's words, 'a noble and puissant nation rousing herself like a strong man after sleep, and shaking her invincible locks.' Without being too crassly figurative one may put the thing in Biblical phrase: 'The winter was past, the rain was over and gone, and the time of the singing of birds had come.' This is no place to linger on the glory of those spacious days. The one thing which I wish to emphasize is this: with the new quickening of every phase of life, the language itself kept even pace. There was a fresh consciousness of its possibilities, a sovereign and masterful exploitation of its hitherto undreamed resources. For the Elizabethans dealt with their speech as they dealt with life — with an adventurous zest in exacting from it all it had to give. 'The lady shall speak her mind freely, or the blank verse shall halt for't,' says Hamlet to the players — and to say its mind freely, to the top of its bent, this particular period proposed; and if the language cabined, cribbed, confined it — why, then, the language must expand! And expand it did, with palpable growing pains now and then, but with an ultimate gain in freshness, in vividness, in raciness, in flexibility which it has never wholly lost. And so far as their medium was concerned, the King James translators fell upon lucky days.

They had at their disposal, then, on its Saxon side, a vocabulary scarcely less concrete and vivid than that of the Hebrew itself. Here is a paragraph from a book printed a hundred years before Shakespeare began to write, but widely read in Shakespeare's day — Malory's *Morte d'Arthur*:

> And as the king lay in his cabin in the ship, he fell in a slumbering, and dreamed a marvellous dream: him seemed that a dreadful dragon did drown much of his people, and he came flying out of the west, and his head was enamelled with azure, and his shoulders shone as gold, his belly like mails of a marvellous hue,

his tail full of tatters, his feet full of fine sable, and his claws like fine gold; and an hideous flame of fire flew out of his mouth, like as the land and water had flamed all of fire. After him seemed there came out of the orient a grimly boar all black in a cloud, and his paws as big as a post; he was rugged looking roughly, he was the foulest beast that ever man saw, he roared and romed so hideously that it were marvel to hear. Then the dreadful dragon advanced him, and came in the wind like a falcon, giving great strokes on the boar, and the boar hit him again with his grisly tusks that his breast was all bloody, and that the hot blood made all the sea red of his blood. Then the dragon flew away all on an height, and came down with such a swough, and smote the boar on the ridge, which was ten foot large from the head to the tail, and smote the boar all to powder, both flesh and bones, that it flittered all abroad on the sea.

There is no lack in that diction of vigour, of concreteness, of picturing power! And when the translators of the Bible came to their task, they found a medium ready to their hand:

Blessed above women shall Jael the wife of Heber the Kenite be, blessed shall she be above women in the tent. He asked water, and she gave him milk; she brought forth butter in a lordly dish. She put her hand to the nail, and her right hand to the workmen's hammer; and with the hammer she smote Sisera, she smote off his head, when she had pierced and stricken through his temples. At her feet he bowed, he fell, he lay down: at her feet he bowed, he fell: where he bowed, there he fell down dead.

Or take another passage from Malory, and one from the Bible again.

Ah, Launcelot, he said, thou were head of all christian knights; and now I dare say, said Sir Ector, thou Sir Launcelot, there thou liest, that thou were never matched of earthly knights' hand; and thou were the courtiest knight that ever bare shield; and thou were the truest friend to thy lover that ever bestrode horse; and thou were the truest lover of a sinful man that ever loved woman; and thou were the kindest man that ever strake with sword; and thou were the goodliest person that ever came among press of knights; and thou was the meekest man and the gentlest that ever ate in hall among ladies; and thou were the sternest knight to thy mortal foe that ever put spear in the rest.

Now hear the other:

The beauty of Israel is slain upon thy high places: how are the mighty fallen! ... From the blood of the slain, from the fat of the mighty, the bow of Jonathan turned not back, and the sword of Saul returned not empty. Saul and Jonathan were lovely and pleasant in their lives, and in their death they were not divided: they were swifter than eagles, they were stronger than lions. ... How are the mighty fallen in the midst of battle! O Jonathan, thou wast slain in thine high places. I am distressed for thee, my brother Jonathan: very pleasant hast thou been unto me: thy love to me was wonderful, passing the love of women. How are the mighty fallen, and the weapons of war perished!

There is in the translation from the Hebrew a majestic rhythm, of which I shall speak later, and which the prose of Malory lacks; but the two agree in the simplicity and the directness of their diction. And those qualities of the native element of English have met and merged with similar, often identical,

qualities of the original. For no less than the Hebrew, the native English is the language of the eye,
the hand, the heart, and one of the supreme merits
of the Jacobean translators is their sense of that
fundamental fact. Let me choose three other brief
passages to make still clearer what I mean:

> Intreat me not to leave thee, or to return from
> following after thee: for whither thou goest, I will go;
> and where thou lodgest, I will lodge: thy people shall
> be my people, and thy God my God: where thou diest,
> will I die, and there will I be buried: the Lord do so
> to me, and more also, if ought but death part thee and
> me.
> Set me as a seal upon thine heart, as a seal upon
> thine arm: for love is strong as death.... Many
> waters cannot quench love, neither can the floods
> drown it: if a man would give all the substance of his
> house for love, it would utterly be contemned.
> And God shall wipe away all tears from their eyes;
> and there shall be no more death, neither sorrow, nor
> crying, neither shall there be any more pain.

There are no nobler passages in English prose.
And out of the 144 words that I have just read, only
ten are not of native origin. And the far-reaching
and pervasive influence of the King James version
of the Bible upon English style is very largely due
to this happy coincidence of qualities in two languages in other respects as far apart as the East is
from the West.

But simplicity is not the only quality of the diction
of the King James version. It has majesty and
stateliness as well. And that lofty grandeur of the

diction of the English Bible is due in large degree
to still another remarkable convergence of kindred
qualities in two otherwise alien tongues. For centuries the ear of English-speaking people had been
attuned to the sonorous diction of the service of the
church — to the majestic Latin of its offices and of
its hymns. And for sheer splendour of verbal music
the Latin of the Church — if I may express my own
opinion — has never been surpassed. Let me read
a brief passage from the lines of Bernard of Cluny
on which the familiar hymn 'Jerusalem the Golden'
is based:

> Urbs Sion aurea, patria lactea, cive decora,
> Omne cor obruis, omnibus obstruis et cor et ora.
> Nescio, nescio, quae jubilatio, lux tibi qualis,
> Quam socialia gaudia, gloria quam specialis. . . .
> Urbs Sion inclyta, turris et edita littore tuto,
> Te peto, te colo, te flagro, te volo, canto, saluto . . .
> O bona patria, num tua gaudia teque videbo?
> O bona patria, num tua praemia plena tenebo? . . .
> Pax ibi florida, pascua vivida, viva medulla,
> Nulla molestia, nulla tragoedia, lacryma nulla.
> O sacra potio, sacra refectio, pax animarum,
> O pius, O bonus, O placidus sonus, hymnus earum.

Or listen to the clangor of this:

> Mortis portis fractis, fortis
> Fortior vim sustulit;
> Et per crucem regem trucem
> Infernorum perculit.
> Lumen clarum tenebrarum
> Sedibus resplenduit;
> Dum salvare, recreare,
> Quod creavit, voluit.

16

Or to the mellower music of this — from the original of the hymn we know as 'Jesus, the very thought of thee':

> Jesu, dulcis memoria
> Dans vera cordis gaudia,
> Sed super mel et omnia
> Eius dulcis praesentia. . . .
>
> Jesu, dulcedo cordium,
> Fons vivus, lumen mentium,
> Excedens omne gaudium,
> Et omne desiderium. . . .
>
> Mane nobiscum, Domine,
> Et nos illustra lumine,
> Pulsa noctis caligine
> Mundum replens dulcedine.

I have read these because I want to make at least reasonably clear the sort of thing that had trained the ear, and had become through generations part and parcel of the subconscious possession of those who listened, even without understanding, to the service of the church. And it was in the majestic Latin of the Vulgate that the Bible, in that service, for centuries was heard. And the sonorousness of the Latin, no less than the simplicity of the Hebrew, found in English its apt and adequate vehicle. For through its enormous Latin element the English vocabulary had become an instrument capable of scarcely less stately harmonies than Latin itself. And so, in the King James Bible, we find the plangent organ music of passages like these:

And after these things I heard a great voice of much people in heaven, saying Alleluia; Salvation, and glory, and honour, and power, unto the Lord our God. . . . And I heard as it were the voice of a great multitude, and as the voice of many waters, and as the voice of mighty thunderings, saying, Alleluia; for the Lord God omnipotent reigneth.

Who shall separate us from the love of Christ? Shall tribulation, or distress, or persecution, or famine, or nakedness, or peril, or sword? . . . Nay, in all these things we are more than conquerors through him that loved us. For I am persuaded, that neither death, nor life, nor angels, nor principalities, nor powers, nor things present, nor things to come, nor height, nor depth, nor any other creature, shall be able to separate us from the love of God, which is in Christ Jesus our Lord.

For this corruptible must put on incorruption, and this mortal must put on immortality. So when this corruptible shall have put on incorruption, and this mortal shall have put on immortality, then shall be brought to pass the saying that is written, Death is swallowed up in victory.

In a word, the supreme qualities of two vocabularies — the Hebrew of the writers of the Bible, and the Latin of its most influential version — found their counterpart in English; and to this complex of correspondences is largely due the marvellous felicity of diction which has made the English Bible a potent factor in the ennobling of the English speech.

But the bare fact of the adaptability of the language is not enough in itself to account for the surpassing beauty of the diction of the King James version. All harmonies (to indulge in a platitude) are latent in the complex mechanism of an organ, but a master's hand is necessary to evoke them. And the existence of a rich and supple medium of expression is not alone enough to make a masterpiece — or even to preclude monstrosities. There is something else which must come into the reckoning. What kept, for example, the Jacobean translators from perpetrating such a prodigy of unbridled diction as Stanyhurst's attempt to render Virgil, printed only thirty years before? Here are a few lines of that ill-starred performance:

And thus as he mused, with tears Venus heauye beblubberd
Prest foorth in presence, and whimpring framed her errand.
O God most pusiaunt, whose mighty auctoritye lasting
Ruls gods, and mankind skeareth with thunderus humbling:
What syn hath Aeneas, my brat, committed agaynst the? . . .

Here is another sample:

For the unsauerye rakhel with collops bludred yfrancked,
With chuffe chaffe wynesops lyke a gourd bourrachoe re-
plennisht,
His nodil in crossewise wresting downe droups to the grownd-
ward,
In belche galp vometing with dead sleape snortye the collops,
Raw with wyne soused, we doe pray toe supernal assemblye,
Round with al embaying thee muffe maffe loller.

That is what became of the beauteous majesty of Virgil under one of the linguistic tendencies of the day. What saved the translation of the Bible from similar disfigurement? Or what kept it from such ridiculous excess as marks the pages of half the fashionable, courtly writing of the period, as one finds it, for example, in a book whose very title is the *reductio ad absurdum* of the vogue: 'A Petite Pallace of Pettie his Pleasure Containing Many Pretie Histories by him set forth in Comely Colours and most Delightfully Discoursed' — in the very first story of which we are to see 'a marvellous mirror of blessed matrimony, and a terrible type of beastly tyranny'? That painful situation comes about, we are told, because 'this Sinorix, glancing his gazing eyes on the blazing beauty of Camma, received so deep an impression of her perfection in his heart, that immediately he fixed his fancy upon her comely corps.' Men were freely indulging in that amazing jargon while the translation of the Bible was under way. What conserved against such influences its unfailing dignity and exquisite felicity of word and phrase? The causes, I think, were chiefly two.

The one is, of course, the loftiness and beauty of the original itself, which tended, through its own compelling influence, to exercise a check upon linguistic eccentricities. But even the depth and beauty of the original, potent a factor as admittedly it was, is not sufficient to account for the freedom of the King James version from disfiguring elements. For there have been notoriously queer translations of this same beautiful original. The noble simplicity of the twenty-third Psalm did not deter Simon Patrick, Lord Bishop of Chichester, who during the 1680's paraphrased both the Psalms and the Song of

Songs, from the exercise of his own peculiar gifts. 'He maketh me to lie down in green pastures; he leadeth me beside the still waters'; that is the second verse as we have it in the King James version. And this is Patrick's paraphrase: 'For as a good Shepherd leads his Sheep in the violent Heat to shady Places, where they may lie down and feed (not in parched, but) in fresh and green Pastures; and in the Evening leads them (not to muddy and troubled Waters, but) to pure and quiet streams: so hath he already made a fair and plentiful Provision for me; which I enjoy in Peace without any disturbance.' Here, again, is one of the lyric cries of the Song of Songs, as the Jacobean translators rendered it: 'I charge you, O daughters of Jerusalem, if ye find my beloved, that ye tell him that I am sick of love.' And this is Simon Patrick's version of the same: 'So I turned myself to those of my Neighbours and familiar Acquaintance, who were awakened by my cries to come and see what the matter was; and conjured them, as they would answer it to God, that if they met with my Beloved, they would let Him know — what shall I say? — what shall I desire you to tell Him? but that I do not enjoy myself, now that I want his Company nor can be well, till I recover his love again.' — 'Whither is fled the visionary gleam? Where is it now, the glory and the dream?' If ever the beauty of Israel was slain upon its high places, it was when Simon Patrick took pen in hand as an improver of the Bible! Even the Rheims version, on which the King James translators drew for some of

their happiest renderings, was capable of such
vagaries as 'Give us to day our supersubstantial
bread,' or 'Beneficence and communication do not
forget, for with such hosets God is promerited'; while
for the great Jacobean phrase 'the deep things of
God' the Rhemish translators read 'the *profundities
of God.*' Obviously even the influence of the great
original was not sufficient to hold in check the eccentricities of individual translators. The reason
for the transcendent merits of the prose diction of
the King James version is found, in large measure, in
another fact.

That fact is this. The 'Authorized' Version repre-
sents a slow, almost impersonal evolution. For it is,
in reality, itself a revision, resting upon earlier ver-
sions, and these, in turn, depend in varying degrees
upon each other, so that through the gradual exercise of something which approaches natural
selection, there has come about, in both diction
and phraseology, a true survival of the fittest. For
the earliest vernacular version in English we must
go back to Wycliffe and his followers, in Chaucer's
day. But the immediate development with which
we are concerned begins with Tyndale, the first
part of whose translation appeared in 1525, almost
a century before the Jacobean version saw the light.
Following Tyndale's translation, at intervals through
the sixteenth century, came five others. In 1535
appeared Coverdale's Bible, a revision of Tyndale,
with the help of the Swiss-German version of 1524–
29, and also of Luther's vivid and idiomatic render-

ing. Next came Matthew's Bible (edited, chiefly
from Tyndale, by that John Rogers with whose
martyrdom the New England Primer has made us
all familiar), and then, in 1539, the Great Bible,
revised by Coverdale from Matthew's Bible. In
1560 the Protestants exiled under Mary made at
Geneva a version, known as the Geneva Bible, based
more closely than the others on the original, but
powerfully influenced still by the work of Tyndale
and Coverdale. In 1568 was published the Bishop's
Bible — itself a revision of the Great Bible, with the
aid of the Geneva version — which, in turn, formed
the ostensible basis of the King James version. And
entering the current to a slight degree is also the
Rhemish Bible, the English translation made by
the Romanists during the 'eighties of the sixteenth
century.

The style of the King James version then is, as
I have said, an evolution. It rests in the first instance upon the translation of John Tyndale; but
it is, in the end, the resultant of a long selective
process, of a winnowing of words that lasted almost
a century. Tyndale's own diction was singularly
simple, energetic, nervous, and yet restrained; the
closing years of the sixteenth century were, as we
have seen, a period of vivid and fresh and plastic
speech; and the long process of impersonal selection,
through the influence of version upon version, served
(to use Dante's phrase) as 'a sieve for noble words.'
And through the influence of the diction which
emerged at last from that complex interplay of

23

varied forces, the current of our speech has been enriched by

> Words that have drawn transcendent meanings up
> From the best passion of all by-gone time,
> Steeped through with tears of triumph and remorse,
> Sweet with all sainthood, cleansed in martyr-fires.

Those lines of Lowell's are literally true. And they lead us at once, with their recognition of an undertone of profound emotion which pervades the history, to another aspect of the subject. For the prose of the Jacobean version is magnificently rhythmic, and its rhythms represent an evolution too.

II

The language of elevated thought or feeling is always rhythmic. Strong feeling of whatever sort, that is, imposes upon speech a rhythmic beat. Even you and I, whose ordinary daily talk maintains its slow or hurried, nervous or phlegmatic, staccato or legato, but always pedestrian gait — even you and I, under stress of compelling emotion find our speech taking on not only deeper colour, but a more or less measured and inevitable beat. That rhythm is not the rhythm of verse; it is infinitely more varied, less susceptible of formulation, ebbing and flowing — sometimes even surging, pulsing, throbbing — with the systole and diastole of the emotion, controlled or unrestrained which gives it birth. And it is that heightening of rhythmic quality, whenever thought is deeply tinged with feeling, that characterizes elevated, as over against purely expository, prose.

Now the Biblical literature, to an almost unrivalled degree, is profoundly tinged with feeling. Racial bent, no less than the drama of their history, led the writers of the Bible to a strongly felt rather than closely reasoned envisagement of life. Caught as their little country was between the upper and nether millstones of the great empires to the north and to the south, mere puppets as they were between the fell incensed points of mighty opposites, the Jewish race faced a terrible enigma, and the great literature of the Exile is little else than a passionate attempt to solve what seemed to be an inexplicable riddle — the mysterious ways of God with men. The Old Testament writings, in the form in which we have them now, date in large measure from that period of stress, and the tragic problem of continued national existence merged — once more in the minds of prophets and poets and chroniclers alike — with the no less tragic spiritual problem of God's enigmatic dealings with his chosen race. No people, perhaps, so deeply felt the burthen of the mystery, the heavy and the weary weight of all this unintelligible world, as did the Jews; and no literature, I think, is so pervaded with profound and passionate emotion as the writings of the Old and the New Testaments.

Nor is that all. There is again a strange and significant parallel. For the century during which the English translation slowly grew, was also a period of great spiritual stress. Tyndale's heroic life ended in martyrdom; John Rogers died at the stake; none of the earlier translators counted their lives dear unto themselves. Translation and original alike came through the furnace, and those who first wrote and those who last rendered were inspired by an intensity of feeling which found inevitable expression, among other ways, in the very cadences of their speech. For the prose of the King James version is not rhythmic without cause. We are dealing, as in the matter of the diction, with a development, and the very mould in which the familiar words are cast — the actual rhythms of the majestic English prose which we have just read — are what they are through influences active for centuries before the Jacobean translators were born.

One of those influences lay in the very nature of Hebrew poetry itself, the formative principle of which, as everybody knows, was what has been called 'the rhythm of meaning' — a parallelism of thought, as well as of form, which was susceptible of infinite variety. ' "The rapid stroke as of alternate wings," ' says Dean Stanley, in a well-known passage, ' "the heaving and sinking as of the troubled heart," which have been beautifully described as the essence of the parallel structure of Hebrew verse, are exactly suited for the endless play of human feeling, and for the understanding of every age and nation.' And again, as in the case of the diction, we have to observe a peculiar circumstance. Poetic rhythms, as a rule, are incorrigibly untranslatable; the luckless fate of innumerable 'translations in the metres of the original' bears eloquent witness to that mournful truth. But here was a rhythm dependent upon an inner impulse rather than upon external rule — ebbing and flowing, rising and falling with the fluctuations of thought or mood, and carrying, through its powerful beat, the impelling emotion into the reader's mind, to stir in turn the springs of rhythm there. The sixteenth- and seventeenth-century translators of the Bible were happily untroubled by pedantic theories of the technique of Hebrew verse; what they felt was this deep inner rhythm — this alternating surge of thought or feeling; and untrammelled by any attempt to reproduce with technical exactness its outward form, they responded to its inner spirit in a prose whose rhythms, so moulded, have a flexibility, a stateliness, a grand freedom, which even the original does not always share. Sometimes it is a majestic march of rhythms like that of an army with banners:

> Hast thou not known? Hast thou not heard, that the everlasting God, the Lord, the creator of the ends of the earth, fainteth not, neither is weary? there is no searching of his understanding. He giveth power to the faint; and to them that have no might he increaseth strength. Even the youths shall faint and be weary, and the young men shall utterly fall. But they that wait upon the Lord shall renew their strength; they shall mount up with wings as eagles; they shall run, and not be weary; they shall walk, and not faint.

Or again, it is precisely that heaving and sinking

as of the troubled heart of which Dean Stanley speaks:

> Why died I not from the womb? why did I not give up the ghost when I came out of the belly? Why did the knees prevent me? or why the breasts that I should suck? For now should I have lain still and been quiet, I should have slept: then had I been at rest, with kings and counsellors of the earth, which built desolate places for themselves; or with princes that had gold, who filled their houses with silver: or as an hidden untimely birth I had not been; as infants which never saw light. There the wicked cease from troubling, and there the weary be at rest. There the prisoners rest together; they hear not the voice of the oppressor. The small and the great are there; and the servant is free from his master.

Now it is in the exquisite swell of a rhythm to its climax:

> For, lo, the winter is past, the rain is over and gone; the flowers appear on the earth; the time of the singing of birds is come, and the voice of the turtle is heard in our land.

Again it is the measured beat of passion in restraint, as in that passage which Professor Saintsbury once singled out as the best example known to him of 'absolutely perfect English prose' — a passage which I have already read in part for the matchless beauty of its diction:

> Set me as a seal upon thine heart, as a seal upon thine arm: for love is strong as death; jealousy is cruel as the grave: the coals thereof are coals of fire,

which hath a most vehement flame. Many waters cannot quench love, neither can the floods drown it: if a man would give all the substance of his house for love, it would utterly be contemned.

Through every one of those passages runs the balanced structure of the Hebrew verse; but it has translated itself into a marvellously rich and varied rhythmic prose which through three centuries — alas! that one should have to add, less potently today — has attuned to its harmonies the English ear, and influenced the noblest English style.

I may not speak at length as I wish I might, of the co-operant influence of the majestic rhythms of Jerome's Latin in the Vulgate. As in the case of the diction, so here again there has been an extraordinary interweaving of disparate strands, and the very order of the English words in some of those passages in the King James version which are most stately in their going, is what it is because of the stamp impressed upon the Vulgate by the powerful personality of Saint Jerome. It would not be impossible to point out sentences in the King James version in which converge, in the present order of the English words, the turns of expression, under strong emotion, of four men living centuries apart — of some nameless writer of the Exile, and of Saint Jerome, John Tyndale, and Miles Coverdale. And you and I echo their dead voices as we read. For not only is the message of the Bible the most profoundly human that was ever penned, but its very form, in the soberest, least sentimental sense, is compact of 'the mighty hopes' — and fears — 'that make us men.'

I may only mention the way in which, from version to version through the century in which the King James version grew, its prose acquired a deepeningly rhythmic quality. 'They shall hunger no more, neither thirst any more.' Compare the cadence of that sentence with the rendering of Wycliffe: 'Thei schulen no more hungre nether thirst.' The change in the order, and the addition of the two words 'any more' — 'They shall hunger no more, neither thirst any more' — have touched Wycliffe's words with new and imperishable beauty. The Bishops' Bible reads: 'He is suche a man as hath good experience of sorowes and infirmities.' The Genevan version changed it to 'a man ful of sorows and hath experience of infirmities.' It was the King James translators who took the final step to the grave beauty of the perfect wording that we know: 'a man of sorrows, and acquainted with grief.' More than to any one else it was to John Tyndale that the noblest qualities of the Biblical prose are due. Yet here is even Tyndale's rendering of the opening verses of Genesis: 'In the begynnynge God created heaven and erth. The erth was voyde and emptie, and darcknesse was upon the depe, and the spirite of god moved upon the water.' That is substantially the version that we know. Yet it lacks the rhythmic grandeur, unobtrusive but pervasive, which the Jacobean rendering has: 'In the beginning God created the heaven and the earth. And the earth was without form, and void; and darkness was upon the face of the deep. And the spirit of God moved upon the face of the waters.' 'Come unto me, all ye who labour and are heavy laden, and I will give you rest,' owes as much to its matchless loveliness of form as it does to the spiritual beauty of its content. If one doubt that, one need only listen to its earliest English rendering: 'Alle ye that traueilen, and ben chargid, come to me, and Y schal fulfille you.'

One could go on for ever; that is enough, I think, to show that the mould in which the well-known phraseology is cast was no happy accident, but the outcome of movements and tendencies rooted deep in racial and personal experience. And in the response of the last three centuries to that great utterance, which has become, with Milton, the 'organ-voice of England,' deep has answered to deep again.

The Pilgrim's Progress

The Pilgrim's Progress

A STUDY IN LITERARY IMMORTALITY

John Bunyan was born in 1628. Just fifty years later, in 1678, *The Pilgrim's Progress* was modestly put forth. And a moment's thought about the world into which it quietly slipped reveals a singular paradox. Consider, in a word, the names which lend glory to English letters in this same seventeenth century. Shakespeare, during its first decade, was at the zenith of his powers. Bacon towers, like Archangel ruined, as its first quarter ends. The closing years of the third saw Milton once for all assume his place with Homer, Virgil, and Dante. Dryden's 'majestic march' held on its stormy way through the last forty years. And John Donne, Ben Jonson, Robert Herrick, Henry Vaughan, Jeremy Taylor, Robert Burton, Sir Thomas Browne, and a score of illustrious names besides, star the intervening years. Yet save for Shakespeare and possibly Milton, the seventeenth-century book most widely read, and through 250 years most universally familiar, was written by an unlearned Puritan preacher, once a tinker, as a dream dreamt in the Bedford gaol. For *The Pil-*

grim's Progress is known not only to everyone who is conversant with the other writings of the period, but to thousands, the world around, who never heard of the *Essays*, or *The Alchemist*, or 'Go and catch a falling star,' or *Hesperides*, or *The Temple*, or *Silex Scintillans*, or the *Anatomy*, or *Religio Medici*, or *All for Love*. It has coloured the imagination and stamped itself upon the phraseology of ten generations of the English-speaking race, and it is read besides in more than one hundred other languages and dialects. What is the secret of an enduring popularity beside which the passing vogues of the best sellers of the day are as a farthing-candle to the sun? I shall have nothing new or startling to bring forward in another of the perennial attempts to find an answer. But the elements of the problem are of deep human interest, and any essay, however unadventurous, at a solution, will bring old facts into fresh juxtapositions. And first a word about the setting of the stage.

For few writers is a study of their temporal background so important and yet at first blush so seemingly irrelevant as in Bunyan's case. For perhaps the most amazing fact about him is his complete isolation from all but one of the great currents of his times. Let me make clear by concrete illustration what I mean. The so-called *Term Catalogues* of the seventeenth and eighteenth centuries are lists of the books published at London in Hilary, Easter, Trinity, and Michaelmas terms each year. The first volume covers the years from 1668 to 1682 —

the period within which fall all but one of Bunyan's four great works. Like its predecessor, the *Stationers' Register*, it is one of the most fascinating documents in the world, and as instructive as it is diverting. And since there is no swifter way to gain a vivid picture of a period than by seeing *en masse* the titles of the books which issued from its press, the *Term Catalogues* offer an expeditious means of reconstructing the background against which *The Pilgrim's Progress* must be thrown. We shall have to confine ourselves to a single year, and even in that to but a handful of its publications. *The Pilgrim's Progress* was printed in Hilary term, 1678. What were some of its associates among the books of that one year?

In that year, for one thing, titles such as these crowd the catalogues: 'The mock *Clelia*; being a Comical History of French Gallantries and Novels'; 'The Heroin Musqueteer, or The Female Warrior. A true History, very delightful and full of pleasant Adventures'; 'Five Love Letters from a Nun to a Cavalier'; 'The Rambling Justice, or The Jealous Husbands'; 'Trick for Trick, or The Debauch'd Hypocrite'; 'The Vice-Roy of *Catalonia*, or the Double Cuckold'; 'The obliging Mistris, or The Fashionable Gallant'; 'The Amorous Convert'; 'Squire *Old Sap*, or the Night Adventures'; 'A pleasant Novel, discovering the Humours and Intrigues of a Town Gallant, in the delectable Amours of *Altophel* and *Astrea*.' And Wycherley's grossly sensual *Plain Dealer* had been published less than a year before. The Restoration, with all its works, was in full swing. And the measure of its remoteness from John Bunyan is afforded by a sentence from his earlier treatise, pleasantly entitled *A Few Sighs from Hell; or, The Groans of a Damned Soul.* The Soul in torment is recalling its past life. Many a time the preacher had told him hell would be his portion, and had urged upon him the reading of the Scriptures. What, alas! had been his fatal answer? 'What is the Scripture? Give me a ballad, a newsbook, George on horseback, or Bevis of Southampton, give me some book that teaches curious arts, that tells of old fables.' And now, as a result, he sighs in hell. One fact, at least, is obvious. The man whose ideas of criminal indulgences in reading were of that pristine innocence moved in a different universe from Mrs. Aphra Behn, or Tom D'Urfey, or William Wycherley, or the authors of 'Delectable Amours' and 'Comical Histories.' *The Pilgrim's Progress* was not carried into favour upon that tide.

Nor was it upon another. One of the strangest things in the world is the way in which great formative currents of thought which are one day to put a different face upon the universe, move quietly on, as it were, through the upper reaches of the atmosphere, while the region below remains as unstirred by their progression as are the leaves of a summer noon by the flow of air which propels the slow-sailing clouds. The seventeenth century, as Professor Whitehead has recently epitomized its genius in a brilliant chapter, was one of the most momentous in the history of human thought. The list of the men who published to the world important work within its limits includes the names of Bacon, Harvey, Kepler, Galileo, Descartes, Pascal, Huygens, Boyle, Newton, Locke, Spinoza, and Leibnitz. It was, beyond doubt, in the field of constructive thought, 'the century of genius.' In England, Bacon had died but two years before Bunyan was born; in the year of Bunyan's birth, William Harvey published his discovery of the circulation of the blood. Newton's *Principia* saw the light the year before Bunyan's death. When *Grace Abounding* was published, the Royal Society was four years old. Robert Boyle was inventing his air-pump in the year that saw *Sighs from Hell*, and was incessantly experimenting through the whole of Bunyan's literary life. Locke's great *Essay concerning Human Understanding* was incubating at the period when *The Pilgrim's Progress* was begun. And the *Term Catalogues* for the year of the allegory's publication list treatise upon treatise, largely sponsored by the vigorous young Royal Society, in the new fields of scientific exploration and discovery. But of the tremendous intellectual adventure of his century, synchronous though it was at every point with his own spiritual pilgrimage, Bunyan could not have been more oblivious had he been a denizen of the moon.

There was, however, a third current which was flowing full and strong. For the nation, if we exclude the men of learning and the circles which centred about the court, it was beyond comparison the widest in its influence of all. The group of books headed 'Divir.'ty' in the *Term Catalogues* is made up largely of sermons — of sermons, for example, on 'The Believer's Groan for Heaven,' '*Achitophel* Befool'd,' 'A Wollen Shroud, or Learn to Dye!' 'Ἔυρηκα! Ἔυρηκα! The Virtuous woman found'; 'Say on! or a seasonable Plea for a full Hearing betwixt man and man.' The godly tractates and pious chansons sometimes have, to be sure, in the *Catalogues*, queer company. 'The History of the Birth, Life, Sufferings, and Death, of our Saviour *Jesus Christ*' succeeds without interval 'The feigned Courtezan, or a night's intreague'; 'A Divine Poem upon *Joseph* and his Brethren' follows at once, with undesigned humour, '*Cytherea*, or the Enamouring Girdle.' Publishers, like Paul, must be all things to all men, that by all means they may reach some. But in the *Catalogue* for Hilary term, secure from corrupting influence under 'Divinity,' and tucked away among the sermons, *The Pilgrim's Progress* stands as the ninth item for the year. It is flanked, on the one side, by 'Μαρτυρολογία ᾽Αλφαβετική, or An Alphabetical Martyrology ... extracted out of Fox's "Acts and Monuments of the Church"'; on the other side by 'The Young Man's Calling, or The whole Duty of Youth. ... Together with Remarks on the Lives of several excellent young Persons, who have been famous for Vertue and Piety. With Sculptures illustrating the several Histories.' It stands, that is, through a curious coincidence, between extracts from the very volumes which Bunyan might have called (as Chaucer called his Ovid) 'myn owene book,' and lives of youthful Christians and Stand-fasts and Faithfuls. And the utter fortuitousness of the juxtaposition lends point to its significance. For through the mid-century, remote alike from Theatre Royal and Royal Society, there flowed a steady stream of books, the end of which, whatever the form, was edification. And the form was often alluring enough. The next title after 'The Young Man's Calling' is this: 'The Sea-man's Spiritual Companion, or Navigation spiritualized. A Poem; being a new Compass for Seamen, consisting of Thirty-two Points, directing every Christian how to stear the Course of his Life through all Storms and Tempests. By W. Balmford.' Bunyan and Balmford have a common theme; only Balmford's Christian is a mariner, and his pilgrimage a voyage. And no less suggestive is a title a few pages farther on: 'A Christian's Walk and Work on Earth until he attain to Heaven; which may serve as a Practical Guide, and a plain direction in his Pilgrimage thither. . . . Marvellously useful to all Persons and Families of all Ranks and Qualities, both in City and Country.' Despite his isolation from the other interests of his times, there was a current, and a strong one, with which Bunyan moved. For *The Pilgrim's Progress*, in its scheme as well as in its object, is not unique. But for us the point of interest is this. 'The Sea-man's Spiritual Companion,' and 'The Christian's Walk and Work on Earth' are dead — as dead as trilobites or door-nails. You may still read them in the British Museum; where else, I do not know. *The Pilgrim's Progress* has been read, and still is read, by millions. It is perennially alive. Why the difference? And now we come at last to Bunyan himself.

Let us waive, temporarily, the accident of genius. Unquestionable as that genius was, the turn which it took was determined to an almost unique degree by the interplay of personality and circumstance. The year of Bunyan's birth saw the Petition of Right and the murder of Buckingham; the year of his death ushered in the Revolution. Between lay the Civil War and the Regicide and the Commonwealth and the Protectorate and the Restoration — then tyranny again. During his lifetime, in a word, England was the theatre of one of the fiercest, most passionate of all the great historic struggles for political and religious liberty. Of the two phases of the conflict, the one caught Bunyan up for a moment, willy-nilly — then dropped him without leaving an appreciable mark; the other first revolutionized, then stamped indelibly, both his inner and his outward life. Of that inner life, the experience described in *Grace Abounding* is for us the crucial point, and I shall deal summarily with the few known antecedent facts.

John Bunyan came of old, free-holding English stock. The Bunyans of his lineage had held land in and about his native village of Elstow in Bedford-shire as early as 1199. He sprang from no upstart or vagrant strain. His father, described in an early document as 'an honest poor labouring man, who, like Adam, unparadised, had all the world before him to get his bread in,' calls himself in his will a 'brasier,' and his son, in his will, designates himself by the same term. Brazier and tinker are one and the same; he was, and his father before him, a maker and mender of pots and kettles, with a workshop and forge at Elstow, and itinerant trade through the countryside. 'My Descent,' he writes in *Grace Abounding*, 'was ... of a low and inconsiderable Generation; my Father's House being of that Rank that is meanest and most despised of all the Families in the Land. ... But yet,' he goes on, ' ... it pleased God to put it into their Hearts to put me to School, to learn both to read and write; the which I also attained, according to the Rate of other poor Men's Children; though to my shame I confess I did soon lose that little I learnt, even almost utterly. ... I had but few Equals,' he continues, ' ... both for cursing, swearing, lying, and blaspheming the holy Name of *God*. ... I was the very Ringleader of all the Youth that kept me company.' From the bare phrase 'When I was a Soldier,' prefixed to an anecdote, it has always been known that he saw military service somewhere. But there is not a word in all his voluminous writings to give a hint of the side on which he fought. For him, after his conversion, Parliament *v*. King stood to God *v*. devil as an anthill to the universe. We know now, from the recently discovered muster-rolls of Newport Pagnell in Buckinghamshire, that he was one of the parliamentary garrison of that town from November, 1644, when he had reached sixteen (the age of compulsory service) until about 1647. The garrison of Newport saw no very active service. Save for stored up recollections later to lend vividness to the allegory of *The Holy War*, the momentous struggle for free institutions seems to have moved John Bunyan not at all. 'Presently after this, I changed,' he writes, 'my Condition into a married State, and my Mercy was to light upon a Wife whose Father was counted godly. This Woman and I' — we do not even know her name — 'though we came together as poor as poor might be (not having so much household stuff as a Dish or Spoon betwixt us both), yet this she had for her part, *The Plain Man's Pathway to Heaven*, and *The Practice of Piety*, which her *Father* had left her when he died. In these two Books I should sometimes read with her ... but all this while I met with no Conviction.' And that brings us to an experience through which we touch the very heart and centre of our problem.

Unless it be certain passages of the *Confessions* of Saint Augustine, I know no human document which reveals with such intensity as *Grace Abounding to the Chief of Sinners* the struggle of a soul in agony. Throughout Augustine's great self-revelation one of the keenest of mortal intellects is at once actor and spectator and consummate analyst of the conflict. In Bunyan's recital, so vividly direct and concrete and intimate is the narrative that one feels as one reads the sheer impact of immediate experience. There are heights and depths in the *Confessions* which *Grace Abounding* never knew. *Quia fecisti nos ad te, et inquietum est cor nostrum, donec requiescat in te:* 'Thou hast made us for Thyself, and our heart is restless, till it rest in Thee' — the majesty of that profound and haunting sentence was out of Bunyan's scope. But in Bunyan's book the daring title of Francis Thompson's record of like experience finds its warrant. For in *Grace Abounding* the Hound of Heaven was on Bunyan's traces, as he 'fled Him, down the nights and down the days.' It must be read entire to feel its power; but a cento of excerpts will give some inkling of its singular quality. And in that quality lies half, but only half, the secret of *The Pilgrim's Progress*.

It is the terrible immediacy of the experience, then, and a directness of speech which sometimes strikes, as Bunyan said of a certain scripture, 'like a hot thunderbolt,' that reveal themselves in the three passages which I have chosen. The document is of a piece; my selections, far from being exceptional, represent its very texture.

The first follows a period of deep despair: 'I found myself as on a miry Bog that shook if I did but stir. . . . I was more loathsome in my own Eyes than was a Toad. . . . I began to entertain such discouragement in my Heart as laid me low as Hell.'

Now about a Week or Fortnight after this, I was much followed by this Scripture, *Simon, Simon, behold, Satan hath desired to have you.* And sometimes it would sound so loud within me, yea, and as it were call so strongly after me, that once above all the rest, I turned my head over my shoulder, thinking verily that some Man had, behind me, called to me; being at a great distance, methought he called so loud ... I thought verily, as I have told you, that somebody had called after me, that was half a Mile behind me; and although that was not my Name, yet it made me suddenly look behind me, believing that he who called so loud meant me. . . .

About the space of a Month after a very great storm came down upon me, which handled me twenty times worse than all I had met with before. It came stealing upon me, now by one piece, then by another; first, all my comfort was taken from me, then darkness seized upon me, after which whole floods of blasphemies ... were poured upon my spirit. . . . These suggestions (with many other which at this time I may not, nor dare not utter, neither by word nor pen), did make such a seizure upon my spirit, and did so overweigh my heart, both with their number, continuance, and fiery force, that I felt as if there were nothing else but these from morning to night within me. . . . In these days, when I have heard others talk of what was the sin against the Holy Ghost, then would the Tempter so provoke me to desire to sin that sin, that I was as if I could not, must not, neither should be quiet until I had committed that. Now, no sin would serve but that; if it were to be committed by speaking of such a word, then I have been as if my Mouth would have spoken that word, whether I would or no; and in so strong a measure was this temptation upon me, that often I have been ready to clap my

hand under my Chin, to hold my Mouth from open-
ing. . . . And now my heart was . . . exceeding hard.
If I would have given a thousand Pounds for a Tear,
I could not shed one.

Then came 'a more grievous and dreadful Temptation than before.'

And that was, *To sell and part with this most blessed
Christ, to exchange him for the things of this life, for any-
thing.* The Temptation lay upon me for the space of a
year, and did follow me so continually that I was not
rid of it one day in a Month, no, not sometimes one
hour in many days together, unless when I was
asleep. . . . I could neither eat my food, stoop for a
pin, chop a stick, or cast mine eye to look on this or
that, but still the temptation would come, *Sell Christ
for this,* or *sell Christ for that; sell him, sell him.*

Sometimes it would run in my thoughts, not so little
as a hundred times together, *Sell him, sell him, sell him;*
against which I may say, for whole hours together, I
have been forced to stand as continually leaning and
forcing my spirit against it . . . that by the very force of
my mind, in labouring to gainsay and resist this
wickedness, my very body also would be put into
action or motion by way of pushing or thrusting with
my hands or elbows, still answering, as fast as the
destroyer said, *Sell him; I will not, I will not, I will not,
I will not; no, not for thousands, thousands, thousands of
Worlds.* . . . But to be brief, one Morning, as I did lie in
my bed, I was, as at other times, most fiercely assaulted
with this temptation, *to sell and part with Christ*; the
wicked suggestion still running in my mind, *Sell him,
sell him, sell him, sell him, sell him,* as fast as a man could
speak. Against which also, in my mind, as at other
times, I answered, *No, no, not for thousands, thousands,
thousands*, at least twenty times together. But at last,

after much striving, even until I was almost out of
breath, I felt this thought pass through my heart, *Let
him go, if he will!* and I thought also, that I felt my
heart freely consent thereto.... Now was the battle
won, and down fell I, as a Bird that is shot from the
top of a tree, into great guilt, and fearful despair....

William James, in *Varieties of Religious Experience*,
classes Bunyan among the 'Sick Souls.' He is that,
at this period, no doubt; the voices and the visions
and the diabolical suggestions and the hound-like
fears are beyond all question psychopathic. But
there is something more. Bunyan did not know it,
but there are elements in his experience which hark
back a thousand years. For so vivid are the hallu-
cinations that one feels, as one reads the thing entire,
behind the Christian phraseology, a sense of something primitive and pagan — of those dark, inscrutable powers that still haunt their ancient
habitations, and lurk, and call, and beckon, and
pursue. When the tempter calls up to Bunyan's
fancy 'the form of a bush, or a bull, or a besom ...
as if I should pray to these,' the old, uncanny shapes,
as we read, for an instant people once more the
fields and cross-roads. Dürer's 'Knight, Death, and
the Devil,' with its fleering, fantastic presences,
might well be the frontispiece of *Grace Abounding* —
except that Dürer's Knight is Mr. Standfast.

But in spite of its poignant human interest, and
in spite of a phraseology which is not so much the
medium of feeling as the live and throbbing thing
itself, *Grace Abounding* is not a familiar book. And

the reason, which bears directly on our question, lies in its very nature. It is molten stuff which is not yet moulded — a profoundly significant human document, but not a work of art. It is intensely personal, but it is not universal. Once impregnate with that sense of immediate personal experience a conception of which the appeal is universal, and a masterpiece is apt to be born. *The Pilgrim's Progress* and *Grace Abounding* have a common theme — the struggle of a human soul. But in *The Pilgrim's Progress* the struggle, still vivid with Bunyan's own remembered experience, has become the Odyssey not of one soul, but of every soul. How did the metamorphosis come about?

In November, 1660, Bunyan was arrested as 'an upholder and maintainer of unlawful conventicles,' and for twelve years lay in the county gaol at Bedford. It was here, before 1666, that *Grace Abounding* was written. In 1672 he was released, and resumed his preaching. In 1675 he was again arrested, and for something under a year was once more a prisoner, this time in the town gaol of Bedford, which stood on the bridge across the Ouse. It was in this 'Denn,' during the second imprisonment, that the First Part of *The Pilgrim's Progress* was conceived. Through the curious irony of things, the immortal tale was a by-product — a fact which Bunyan tells us himself in the lively and artless lines of 'The Author's Apology for his Book':

> When at the first I took my Pen in hand,
> Thus for to write; I did not understand

That I at all should make a little Book
In such a mode; Nay, I had undertook
To make another, which when almost done,
Before I was aware, I this begun.
  And thus it was: I writing of the Way
And Race of Saints, in this our Gospel-Day,
Fell suddenly into an Allegory
About their Journey, and the way to Glory,
In more than twenty things, which I set down;
This done, I twenty more had in my Crown,
And they again began to multiply,
Like sparks that from the coals of fire do fly.
Nay, then, thought I, if that you breed so fast,
I'll put you by yourselves, lest you at last
Should prove *ad infinitum*, and eat out
The Book that I already am about.
  Well, so I did . . . and so I penn'd
It down; until at last it came to be
For length and breadth the bigness which you see.

It is easy to guess what book it was which all at once in its pedestrian pace was startled by a sudden consciousness of wings. Just after his release from gaol the second time, Bunyan published *The Strait Gate; or, Great Difficulty of Going to Heaven*. And as the treatise is drawing to a close, he sets down a series of trenchant little sketches — miniature characters of a dozen types of 'professors' (as he calls them), who enter upon the race, but fail to reach the gaol. They are, in fact, caustic prefigurings, lacking only names, and legs and tongues to walk and talk with, of Mr. By-ends, Mr. Legality, Mr. Talkative, and others of their breed, in the narrative soon to be. All at once, as the picturesque sentences were penned, the conception, implied in the tractate's very title, of the road and the types who travel it, sprang into vivid, concrete form in Bunyan's mind. Like *The Rime of the Ancient Mariner*, it 'grew and grew'; and outgrowing its didactic setting, cut loose and became a masterpiece. And now I come back to the question with which we started: What is the secret of its enduring hold upon generation after generation of its readers?

There is one literary type, and only one, to which the ancient *quod semper, quod ubique, quod ab omnibus* — acceptance always, everywhere, by everybody — incontestably applies. That is the *story*, and *The Pilgrim's Progress* is above all things else a tale. More than that, it is a tale of wayfaring and adventure, with a flavour of old romance — giants and highwaymen and caves and castles and haunted valleys and enchanted grounds — the most irresistible combination in the world. Moreover, it has in high degree that enchanting trait which lends fascination to the folk tale and *Alice in Wonderland* and a dream — the perpetual telescoping of the familiar with the strange. We find ourselves in a bolted dungeon, the prisoners of an authentic chap-book giant and his wife, or alone on a perilous sword-edge pathway, dark as pitch, among doleful voices and rushings to and fro of Hobgoblins and Satyrs and Dragons of the Pit — and we have come on them without surprise by way of pleasant English lanes and meadows, and upon crossing over English stiles. It is all as matter-of-course and as unexpected as a fairy-tale. Furthermore, along the King's High-way and down the green lanes and through the streets of Vanity Fair move living men, however named, who meet and pass and talk and argue and dispute, in the fresh and vivid idiom of the English countryside. And running through the narrative, charged with deep feeling, is a symbolism, simple and straightforward, which lifts it, still indefeasibly a story, into yet another realm of universal human interest.

The story begins with a scene which one some-times feels is unsurpassed in fiction for sheer graphic power:

> As I walk'd through the wilderness of this world, I lighted on a certain place, where was a Den; and I laid me down in that place to sleep: and as I slept I dreamed a Dream. I dreamed, and behold *I saw a man cloathed with Rags, standing in a certain place, with his face from his own House, a Book in his hand, and a great burden upon his back.* I looked, and saw him open the Book, and read therein; and as he read, he wept and trembled: and not being able longer to contain, he broke out with a lamentable cry; saying, *What shall I do?*
>
> I saw also that he looked this way, and that way, as if he would run; yet he stood still, because as I per-ceived he could not tell which way to go. I looked then, and saw a Man named *Evangelist* coming to him, and asked, *Wherefore doest thou cry?* He answered, Sir, I perceive, by the Book in my hand, that I am con-demned to die, and after that to come to Judgement; and I find that I am not willing to do the first, nor able to do the second.

Then after swift question and answer, Evangelist gives him a Parchment-roll.

> The Man therefore read it, and looking upon *Evangelist* very carefully; said, Whither must I fly? Then said *Evangelist*, pointing with his finger over a very wide Field, Do you see yonder *Wicket-gate*? The Man said, No. Then said the other, Do you see yonder shining light? He said, I think I do. Then said *Evangelist*, Keep that light in your eye, and go up directly thereto, so shalt thou see the Gate; at which, when thou knockest, it shall be told thee what thou shalt do.
>
> So I saw in my Dream, that the Man began to run; now he had not run far from his own door, but his Wife and Children perceiving it, began to cry after him to return: but the Man put his fingers in his Ears, and ran on, crying, Life, Life, Eternal Life: so he looked not behind him, but fled towards the middle of the Plain.

No opening that I know cuts straighter and more swiftly to the core, or sets a scene before the eyes with such compelling visualization. Let me repeat five lines of it, which epitomize the quality that penetrates the book:

> The Man therefore read it, and looking upon *Evangelist* very carefully; said, Whither must I fly? Then said *Evangelist*, pointing with his finger over a very wide Field, Do you see yonder *Wicket-gate*? The Man said, No. Then said the other, Do you see yonder shining light? He said, I think I do.

That is not description; it is the thing itself. A man intently reading a roll; the lifting of his eyes to scrutinize another man; the pointing finger; the wicket-gate; the shining light; the anxious travelling of the eye across the field and back again to the pointing finger, and once more peeringly across the field and back again — was there ever, I wonder, another passage into which, within such brief compass, so many visual impressions have been packed? It is easy to say what a thing is *like*, and thousands have the trick. Direct vision, with the power of evoking it in us, is the gift of few, and among them are the greatest. Bunyan has it, and it is with his unswerving intensity of vision that we see: 'Behold I saw'; 'I looked, and saw'; 'I saw also'; 'as I perceived'; 'I looked then, and saw'; 'So I saw in my Dream.' It is no wonder that the pictures live and breathe. And one reason why the book itself has lived is a reason which it shares with *The Divine Comedy* and the *Iliad* and the *Odyssey*, and a hundred passages in Shakespeare (to name no more) — the power of striking out, in a few naked, simple words, a picture which is ineffaceable.

Stevenson has a pertinent paragraph in *A Gossip on Romance*. 'The threads of a story,' he remarks, 'come from time to time together and make a picture in the web. . . . Crusoe recoiling from the footprint, Achilles shouting over against the Trojans, Ulysses bending the great bow, Christian running with his fingers in his ears, these are each culminating moments in the legend, and each has been printed on the mind's eye for ever. . . . This,' he goes on, 'is the highest and hardest thing to do in words; the thing which, once accomplished, equally delights the schoolboy and the sage, and makes, in its own right, the quality of epics.' That in the main is true. But for Bunyan, I think, this *hardest* thing to do in words was the *only* thing to do. So intense and so dramatic was his visualizing energy that he participates in every bodily movement of his characters. That is why his pictures, with their utter simplicity, give the effect of things in three dimensions. We get the sense of movement; we feel obscure muscular responses; we begin ourselves to live in the characters, sharing in our own person their experiences. For myself, I know nothing quite like it.

> Then *Christian* pulled [the Key] out of his bosom, and began to try at the Dungeon door, whose bolt (as he turned the Key) gave back, and the door flew open with ease. ... After he went to the *Iron* Gate, for that must be opened too, but that Lock went *damnable* hard, yet the Key did open it; then they thrust open the Gate to make their escape with speed. ...
>
> Now a little before them, there was on the left hand of the Road, a *Meadow*, and a Stile to go over into it, and that *Meadow* is called *By-Path-Meadow*. Then said *Christian* to his fellow, If this Meadow lieth along by our way side, lets go over into it. So he went to the Stile to see, and behold a Path lay along by the way on the other side of the fence. 'Tis according to my wish said *Christian*, here is the easiest going; come, good *Hopeful*, and let us go over. ... So *Hopeful* ... went after him over the Stile. ...
>
> So *Watchful* the *Porter* rang a Bell, at the sound of which came out at the door of the House a grave and beautiful Damsel, named *Discretion*, and asked why she was called.

That last is the stock scene of a hundred romances, touched with a dignity and beauty which none of them possess, but alive with movement in every phrase. And one of my own most vivid childhood recollections is that of another figure of folk-lore and romance — the impotent old Giant at the end of the Valley,

> ... grown so crazy, and stiff in his joints, that he can now do little more than sit in his Cave's mouth, grinning at Pilgrims as they go by, and biting his nails, because he cannot come at them.

But even that picture yields in graphic intensity to this:

> *Then Apollyon straddled quite over the whole breadth of the way,* and said, I am void of fear in this matter, prepare thyself to die, for I swear ... that thou shalt go no further, here will I spill thy soul.

And as for Christian,

> I never saw him all the while give so much as one pleasant look, till he perceived that he had wounded *Apollyon* with his two edged Sword, then indeed he did smile, and look upward: but *'twas the dreadfullest sight that ever I saw.*

John Bunyan had fought Apollyon too. And that brings us back for a moment to *Grace Abounding*.

For, in effect, *The Pilgrim's Progress* is *Grace Abounding* recollected in tranquillity. The sense of sheer, almost palpable reality which pervades it as no other allegory is pervaded in the world, has its springs in the intensity of those agonizings along the roads and in the fields and under the hedge-rows of Bedfordshire. But that vividness of direct experience is now bathed, as it were, in a broad serenity like that of a race remembered when the immortal garland has been won. Let me illustrate from the setting of the story what I mean.

There is a trick of the brain with which everyone is familiar. Things come back to our memory steeped in the associations of the moment when they were experienced, and suffused with the feelings which the old associations have stirred — as I, for example, can never think of a certain Cornish field-path without feeling the air pervaded with the cuckoo's haunting call. And through the feeling so awakened, the picture which we paint or the incident which we set down, even though no out-ward and visible sign betray the influence, will pos-sess a colour, a vibrancy, an emotional *potential*, which they could never otherwise have had. Now the stage of Bunyan's fierce spiritual conflict had been the English countryside and the life of its rural hamlets — the village green, the church steeple with the bells of his love and terrified renunciation, a shop-window, a settle in the street, the spinsters and the knitters in the sun, footpaths and stiles, crows in a ploughed field, the country lanes, the cottage fire. Could these ever come back to his memory untinged with a dream-like vividness which still invests their homely, familiar actuality with something of the strangeness of another world? In particular, for a period of years, the roads and the by-paths of Bedfordshire had been haunted for him by invisible, importunate presences. Could he ever later walk along these roads without a flood of recollection? Experience of such poignancy as his stamps its setting indelibly upon the brain, and even when tranquillity has been attained, if, at whatever summons, the old setting comes back again to memory, it comes charged with the latent intensity of the original experience. That is why, in *The Pilgrim's Progress*, the story and the landscape — stiles and meadows and wicket-gates and crooked lanes — melt into one another in a harmony almost unique: a harmony pre-established years before on English country roads, which still holds unbroken through the pilgrimage by Doubting Castle and Broadway Gate and Dead Man's Lane and Bypath Meadow and the Enchanted Ground.

But the names which I have just recalled have a double bearing, for they bring us at once to the core of the book, to wit, the allegory. And allegory, for the last hundred years or so, has been the pet aversion of the great majority of English readers. Yet in spite of its antiquated form, *The Pilgrim's Progress* has held serenely on its way. And it is possible, I think, to see the reason of the paradox.

The trouble with most allegories is that their analogies are either strained, or confused, or both. The symbol and the thing symbolized are apt to be more different than alike. The soul and a castle are both subject to attack, and so far forth a castle may and does legitimately symbolize the soul. But the soul has neither barbican nor moat nor draw-bridge, and a castle neither affections nor volitions nor ideas. To force the analogy beyond the common element is to shatter all illusion of reality. And that nine allegories out of ten efficiently accomplish. Moreover, we object, not to symbols in themselves, but to a set of symbols carrying on a complicated action, and behaving now as symbols, now as the objects symbolized. We open, for example, the first canto of *The Faerie Queene*, and before we know it, we are captivated by a lovely damsel in distress, and are thrilled by the adventure of the Red Cross Knight with the loathly monster in the cave, and observe with concern the devilish machinations of an enchanter masquerading as a pious hermit of the dale, and are left, as the canto ends, in a state of delicious suspense: Will or will not the knight believe that the wanton in Una's form who comes to his bed is Una? So far, so good; we have embarked, it would seem, on an uncommonly engaging tale. Then we turn back to the expository quatrain, and we read:

> The patrone of true Holinesse
> Foule Errour doth defeate:
> Hypocrisie, him to entrappe,
> Doth to his home entreate.

And Una has ceased to be Una, and the monster a monster, and the enchanter an enchanter, and they are instead, all three, personified abstractions, behaving as they do because at one moment they are thought of as a lovely lady and a monster and a sorcerer, and at another as Holiness and Error and Hypocrisy. And that maddening play of tele-scoping personalities goes on through not one canto only, but seventy-two. Is anybody in the allegory at any given moment, what he *is*, or what he *seems*? And which in Heaven's name, we ask, is which?

Now the allegory in *The Pilgrim's Progress* is to the allegory in *The Faerie Queene* as a right line is to a labyrinth. The book is as simple and straight-forward as its title-page: 'The Pilgrim's Progress from this World to that which is to come, delivered under the similitude of a Dream. Wherein is dis-covered the Manner of his Setting out, his Danger-ous Journey, and Safe Arrival at the desired Country.' The allegory springs from, pursues un-swervingly, and ends, in one conception, and that as ancient and as universal as mankind. A road, and a dangerous journey, and at the end a shining city paved with gold — that is a theme which for ages has captivated all sorts and conditions of men; and when the road and the journey and the fair city at the journey's end are linked with the theme of a *pilgrimage*, the symbolism, deepened through centuries of associations, becomes instantly and universally intelligible. Nor is this instant intelli-gibility true of the pilgrimage alone. Throughout the allegory Bunyan draws his symbols from objects which, through long and intimate use and wont, have been saturated with symbolic value, or which in themselves are adapted to symbolic use. The symbolism is inherent, not devised. And the sense of utter familiarity with which the allegory is pervaded springs from these old and homely and inevitable emblems, as they in turn have their roots in that imagery in which Bunyan's mind was steeped — the inexhaustible symbolism of the Bible. Bunyan's allegory, unlike Spenser's, is 'understanded of the people,' because its symbols embody the vision, through succeeding generations, of simple, yet imaginative minds. They are as inevitable as the parables.

And in what words of pellucid beauty are the symbols often phrased! The Shining Ones, the 'very stately Palace, the name of which was Beautiful,' the House of the Interpreter, the Delectable Mountains, the 'high Hill, called Clear,' the Land of Beulah, the 'grave and beautiful Damsel named Discretion,' Mr. Great-heart, Mr. Stand-fast, Mr. Valiant-for-Truth. Like a dozen others — the Slough of Despond, the Hill called Difficulty, Vanity Fair, By-Path-Meadow, Doubting Castle, Giant Despair, the Man with the Muck-rake, the Enchanted Ground — they have ever since been current coin, a parcel of the common stock of English phraseology, as familiar as the turns of speech of Shakespeare and the Bible. And this aptness in the coinage of symbolic designations plays an undoubted part in the wide popularity of the allegory. For what we call the general public delights and always has delighted in symbolic phrases. If we think we have outgrown them, we are fooled. Even our own would-be sophisticated generation revels in them. Titles such as these, recalled at random, belong to the worldly-wise, disillusioned period since the 'nineties: The Wings of a Dove, The Golden Bowl, The Ivory Tower, The Candle of Vision, The Glittering Gate, Heart Break House, The Land of Heart's Desire, The Song of the Lark, The Undying Fire. And here, culled from many, are a few titles from the advertising section of a single number of a periodical of the current year: The House of Sun-goes-Down, The Eternal Moment, The Stranger at the Feast, The Island Within, The River Between, The Burning Bush, The Road to Heaven. It is perfectly true that nowadays we fight shy of formal allegory. Responsiveness to symbolism, on the other hand, is bred in the bone. And in his symbolic phraseology Bunyan is as modern as the fiction of 1928.

Moreover, in the exacting art of characterization he rivals and sometimes outstrips the masters, in their own technique. I have of late, I need scarcely say, been re-reading Bunyan, and at the same time, as it happens, Trollope, and Hardy, and Conrad, and a host of smaller fry. All at once, to my amazement, I realized this: barring Hardy's rustics, the people whom I heard talking, saw gesturing, felt as almost bodily presences, as they came unsummoned back to memory, were a dozen or so of Bunyan's pilgrims. Why should allegorical figures, with quaint, sometimes outlandish names, behave in this disconcerting fashion? Well, the quaint abstractions are, to be sure, the vehicles of allegory;

but the one thing which, in Bunyan's hands, they cannot do, is to remain lay figures. Before we know it, they take the allegory in their teeth, and miraculously keeping it from dropping, go serenely their own gait. Except for occasional homiletic divagations, there is nothing remote or tenuous about them. And unlike Spenser's figures, once determined, they 'stay put.' They are palpable flesh and blood, and they talk — and talk in character — like people, not like books. English comedy lost a master when Bunyan was born Puritan.

> HON. *But stay, now you talk of her, methinks I have either seen her, or have read some story of her.*
> STANDFAST. Perhaps you have done both.
> HON. *Madam Bubble? Is she not a tall comely Dame, something of a swarthy Complexion?*
> STANDFAST. Right, you hit it, she is just such an one.
> HON. *Doth she not speak very smoothly, and give you a Smile at the end of a Sentence?*
> STANDFAST. You fall right upon it again; for these are her very Actions.
> HON. *Doth she not wear a great Purse by her Side, and is not her Hand often in it, fingering her Mony, as if that was her Heart's delight?*
> STANDFAST. 'Tis just so. Had she stood by all this while you could not ... have better described her Features.

I am killing two birds with one stone, for the easy, colloquial turn of the dialogue is as masterly as the progressive delineation of the character. And Bunyan had the telling combination at his fingers' tips. His dialogue, in a play, would be the delight of actors. It was *heard*, every word and inflexion of it, as it was written down. The eye on the page misses half of it; it is the ear to which it speaks. Listen!

> CHRISTIAN. *Well then, did you not know about ten years ago, one* Temporary *in your parts, who was a forward man in Religion then?*
>
> HOPEFUL. Know him! Yes, he dwelt in *Graceless*, a Town about two miles off of *Honesty*, and he dwelt next door to one *Turn-back*.
>
> CHRISTIAN. *Right, he dwelt under the same roof with him.*

There in six lines is a compendium of the art — or is it art at all, but Nature? — which gives to Bunyan's allegory instant verisimilitude. 'Know him? Yes!' — and who can longer doubt Temporary's tangible, corporeal existence? Graceless and Honesty *in vacuo* are thin, phantasmal regions, unlocalized and uninhabited. 'Graceless, a Town about two Miles off of Honesty' is *there*; you can find it on the map. And you can live next door to one another in it, and it has houses in which two families live under the same roof. And again the consummate naturalness of the dialogue carries conviction with it. No abstractions ever born could achieve that vivid, idiomatic raciness, and stay abstract. Their blood is nourished on English beef and ale, and they learned to talk in village inns and along the country lanes.

> GREATHEART. *Well said,* Father Honest, *quoth the Guide, for by this I know thou art a Cock of the right kind. . . . Well, now we are so happily met, pray let me crave your Name, and the name of the Place you come from.*

HON. My Name I cannot, but I came from the Town of *Stupidity*; it lieth about four Degrees beyond the City of *Destruction*.

GREATHEART. *Oh! Are you that Countryman then? I deem I have half a guess of you, your name is old* Honesty, *is it not?* So the old Gentleman blushed, and said, Not Honesty in the *abstract*, but *Honest* is my Name, and I wish that my *Nature* shall agree to what I am called.

Once more, these immortal rustics and soldiers and citizens of little towns are no conventional puppets of an allegory. Is Mr. Feeble-mind, who was the nephew of Mr. Fearing, a marionette? 'He was mine Uncle, my Father's Brother; he and I have been much of a Temper, he was a little shorter than I, but yet we were much of a Complexion.' And so close is the resemblance that Mr. Honest sees it: 'You have his whitely Look, a Cast like his with your Eye, and your Speech is much alike.' And that 'very brisk Lad' whose name was Ignorance, and who came down 'a little crooked Lane into the way in which the Pilgrims walked,' is no abstraction; nor is Mr. Talkative, who was the son of one Saywell, and dwelt in Prating-row, and was 'a very pretty man' — 'a tall Man, and something more comely at a distance than at hand'; nor are the three friends of Mr. By-ends, who, being 'a Gentleman of good Quality,' made them 'a very low *Congee*' — 'men that Mr. *By-ends* had formerly been acquainted with, for in their minority they were schoolfellow, and were taught by one Mr. *Gripe-man*, a Schoolmaster in *Love-gain*, which is a

market town in the County of *Coveting* in the North';
nor is that 'very arch Fellow,' Mr. By-ends himself,
the flower of them all. But for me, I confess, the
most engaging of the company is that quartet of
truants from a nursery-tale, who slip unheralded
and undescribed across the narrative and disap-
pear — 'a young Woman her name was *Dull*,' who
abandoned the narrow path with Short-wind and
Slow-pace and Sleepy-head.

There are bits here and there that are worthy of
the contemporary comedy of manners — scenes like
the party at the house of Mrs. Timorous, where
Mrs. Bats-eyes, Mrs. Inconsiderate, Mrs. Light-
mind, and Mrs. Know-nothing meet to discuss
Christiana's setting out for the Celestial City, and
where Mrs. Light-mind, bored to death with serious
discourse, launches into a piquant account of the
dance the day before at Madame Wanton's, where,
with Mrs. Filth and Mr. Lechery, they were 'as
merry as the Maids.' There is talk which might
have fallen from the lips of Joseph Poorgrass or
Thomas Leaf:

> Then said the poor man, I am a sickly man, as you
> see. . . . I am a man of no strength at all of Body, nor
> yet of Mind. . . . I am, as you see, but of a *feeble
> Mind*. . . . I am a very ignorant Christian man.

Old Honest, at once bluff and mellow, consistently
and delightfully in character, the most individual
of all the pilgrims, is somebody of whom Fielding or
Trollope, had either of them conceived him, might

be proud. And English fiction can show few triumphs of characterization which outshine Mr. Great-heart's epitome of Mr. Fearing's pilgrimage. William Vaughn Moody was right: '*The Pilgrim's Progress* was in a very deep sense the first English novel. It sprang racy of the soil: it had its root in daily fact, and drew its sap from the immediately human.'

And that soil was the soil of Bunyan's own Bedfordshire, and the facts were the facts of his intimate knowledge. The setting of the allegory is as true to life as are the characters, and the more one knows of seventeenth-century England, the more one marvels at its verisimilitude. The stately English country houses of which the House called Beautiful is the glorified counterpart; the roadside inns; the roads themselves, with their miry sloughs and lurking highwaymen; the crowded fairs of the market towns, laid out in rows and streets; the spectacle of men shut up in an iron cage; the unjust judges and packed juries — there is none of these of which Bunyan had not had direct experience. Sometimes his use of contemporary incident lacks little of being a sheer transcript of reality, as in that lively anecdote which Christian tells (apropos of 'a very dark Lane' which he and Hopeful happened to be passing) of Little-Faith's adventure with the three robbers at the point where Dead-man's Lane comes down from Broad-way-gate. Turn the pages, sometime, of that most engrossing and improper volume, Captain Charles Johnson's *Lives and Adventures of the Most*

*Famous Highwaymen, Murderers, Street-Robbers, etc. . . .
Interspersed with several diverting Tales, and pleasant
Songs,* and read the careers of such notorious rogues
of Bunyan's day as Claude du Vall, The Golden
Farmer, Old Mobb, Mul-sack, Thomas Dun, born
between Elstow and Kempston, Jacob Halsey, the
son of a Quaker family in Bedford, and you will
cherish no doubt that Christian's tale rehearsed an
actual occurrence. But oftener, the setting is not so
much a transcript as it is a transformation of reality;
as when this or that bit of Bedfordshire landscape
all at once *shines*, with that peculiar detached brightness which belongs to familiar objects seen mir-
rored in a convex glass, or remembered after a vivid
dream. And again and again, as in those rapturous
passages through which peal Bunyan's long forgone
but still beloved bells, one feels the heightening
touch of personal experience.

Even the giants and hobgoblins, and the monster
with wings like a dragon and scales like a fish are
true, in a different but very real sense, to that experience. They are true, in a word, to that immemorial world of wonder and terror which still
lives and has lived for uncounted centuries, as
reality, in simple and unlettered minds. In his
childhood it had 'scared and affrighted' Bunyan,
waking and in dreams, 'with the apprehensions of
devils and wicked spirits.' One still feels it, as I
have said, as a dimly lurking background in *Grace
Abounding*, and in *The Pilgrim's Progress* Bunyan,
now with complete detachment, employs it with

deliberate art. The devils and the fiends had merged, too, with other ingredients. The fascinating story of the strange survivals in Bunyan's century of the disintegrated elements of the great romances is far too long for even the briefest summary here. Sir Charles Firth, in the best introduction to *The Pilgrim's Progress* ever written, was the first to recognize its purport, and on that hint Professor Harold Golder, ransacking the varied lore into which the splendid cycles of romance had broken down, has shown how Bunyan's mind was permeated by the atmosphere and stored with the incidents of the chivalric tales which, on his own testimony, he had read or heard. And man-eating giants and fire-breathing dragons blend in the allegory, as they blended in his mind, with that known and familiar landscape which had once for him been peopled with far more dreadful presences.

But in *The Pilgrim's Progress* the giants and the dragons are but the means of calling forth the staunch and steadfast and great-hearted qualities of living men. And nothing in the allegory gives with such finality the illusion of simple, hearty, native flesh and blood, as does its speech, which, like the rest, is racy of the English soil. There is nothing abstract or allegorical in its occasional robust inelegance. Christiana and the children, after panting up the hill Difficulty 'were all in a pelting heat.' Through the 'dirt and slabbiness' of the Enchanted Ground, with 'grunting and puffing ... they made a pretty good shift to wag along.' From the smoke of the Pit in the Valley, 'behold great stinks and loathesome smells.' When Pliable fell into the Slough of Despond, 'he was soundly bedabbled with that kind of dirt.' That is one side of the shield; here is the other. Christiana and Mercy are at the House called Beautiful:

> MERCY. Hark, don't you hear a Noise?
> CHRIS. Yes, 'tis as I believe, a Noise of Musick, for joy that we are here.
> MERCY. Wonderful! Musick in the House, Musick in the Heart, and Musick also in Heaven, for joy that we are here.

I shall add no words, even of Bunyan's, to mar that loveliness.

Without, then, ever losing its simplicity or its fresh and vigorous idiomatic virtue, Bunyan's language is an instrument of many stops. I do not believe that its flexibility as a medium of characterization has ever been sufficiently observed. Mr. By-ends uses to perfection the smug lingo of the leading citizen of a provincial town; old Honest's talk is as forthright and as reticently warm-hearted as that amiable personage himself; Mr. Feeble-mind's doting garrulousness is done to the life; Mr. Great-heart talks plain soldier:

> Then said Mr. *Great-heart* to Mr. *Valiant-for-truth* (for he loved one greatly that he found to be a man of his Hands), *Thou hast worthily behaved thyself; let me see thy Sword.* So he shewed it him. When he had taken it in his Hand, and looked thereon a while, he said, Ha! *It is a right* Jerusalem *Blade.*

And it was Mr. Great-heart who said of Christian and Faithful:

> But what do we talk of them, they were a couple of Lion-like men; they had set their Faces like Flint.

But for consummate truth to nature there are few things of its sort which rival this:

> Thus they went on till they came to about the middle of the Valley, and then *Christiana* said, Methinks I see something yonder upon the Road before us, a thing of such a shape such as I have not seen. Then said *Joseph*, Mother, what is it? An ugly thing, Child; an ugly thing, said she. But Mother, what is it like, said he? 'Tis like I cannot tell what, said she. And now it was but a little way off. Then said she, it is nigh.
>
> Well, well, said Mr. *Great-heart*, let them that are most afraid keep close to me. So the *Fiend* came on.

The economy of effort with which the tense, hushed dialogue between the mother and the child leads up to that inimitably indulgent and benign reassurance, and the utter simplicity and commonplaceness of every word, are Bunyan when his art is one with nature. And one reason why, instead of shunning his *dramatis personae* as dull abstractions, we find ourselves hobnobbing with them as old friends, lies in the fact that we hear them talking, not with the devastating monotony of creatures who must be always honest, or hopeful, or pliable, or what not, but in different fashions under different moods — even as you and I. Mercy, whose exquisite words in the House called Beautiful we have already heard, speaks once more in perfect character in the Valley of Humiliation:

> Then said *Mercy*, I think I am as well in this Valley, as I have been anywhere else in all our Journey. The place methinks suits with my Spirit. I love to be in such places where there is no rattling with Coaches, nor rumbling with Wheels. . . . Here one may think, and break at Heart, and melt in one's Spirit until one's Eyes become like the *Fish Pools of Heshbon*.

But even the gentle Mercy can blaze out like a woman of the Revolution, so that one feels in her words a different timbre, and the very rhythm of her speech takes on a quickened gait. 'No, no,' she cries, when she sees the bodies of Simple and Sloth and Presumption hanging:

> *No, no, let them hang, and their Names Rot, and their Crimes live forever against them. I think it a high favour that they were hanged afore we came hither, who knows else what they might a done to such poor women as we are?* Then she turned it into a Song, saying,

> > *Now then you three, hang there and be a Sign*
> > *To all that shall against the Truth combine.*

So Deborah — but with a magnificence beyond Mercy's reach — sang of the dead Sisera.

In a word, when Bunyan is at his best — and that is in the lively give and take along the road — like every born novelist or dramatist, he is inside his characters' skins. And his diction takes its colour and its pattern, not from the conventions of some allegorical exemplar, but from what goes on under given conditions in the brain which for the nonce he inhabits. Which is only to say again that in certain supreme essentials *The Pilgrim's Progress* is not far from the kingdom of great fiction.

And quite apart from its dramatic fitness, the diction of *The Pilgrim's Progress* is in itself a perennial delight. I have said nothing of *The Holy War*, and *Mr. Bad-man*, and *The Jerusalem Sinner Saved*, and *A Few Sighs from Hell*, and *The Heavenly Footman*, and the delightful *Book for Boys and Girls*. They are all of a piece, however, in one respect. The same vivid, pithy, homespun diction, especially in narrative and dialogue, weaves the texture of them all. It is the speech to which Bunyan was born and bred — the unlettered language of the youths who played with him at cat, and of the cottagers and the tinkers and the small tradesfolk whom he knew in Elstow, and under the hedgerows, and on the ale-bench at village inns. That in his later years he read much more widely than is commonly supposed, I have myself no doubt. But one of the happiest accidents for English letters was the fact that this reading came too late to sap the vigour of a diction and an idiom which drew their freshness from the native springs of English speech. And happier still is the further fact that the one book which Bunyan knew until his mind was saturated with its phraseology, was the English Bible. Add genius to that unique conjunction, and the phraseology of *The Pilgrim's Progress*, so far as such miracles are susceptible of explanation, stands explained.

I have said nothing of the deep spiritual sincerity of the allegory, and I shall say but little now. It is the supreme source of the book's immortality, but its beauty is best served by reticence. It is enough that in the central embodiment of that sincerity, the story is still true to life. For behind the person of Christian stands the lovable figure of Bunyan himself. One so often wishes that in the allegories the good died young. Their irritating faultlessness is sometimes more than frailer clay can bear. But Christian, like the rest of us, is a faulty, blundering, struggling mortal — despairing, yet doggedly pressing on; afraid, yet fighting like a lion; forgetful, inattentive, easily deceived, retracing painfully false steps — and then, once more, face forward to the goal. He is Mr. Feeble-mind and Mr. Fearing and Mr. Ready-to-halt, but he is also Mr. Great-heart and Mr. Standfast and Mr. Valiant-for-Truth. Had *The Pilgrim's Progress* nothing else than that one great personality to offer, it would still be a book that the world would not willingly let die.

The Art of Geoffrey Chaucer

The Art of Geoffrey Chaucer

MY SUBJECT, as I have announced it, is a theme for a volume, but titles can seldom be brief and specific at once. I mean to limit myself to an attempt to answer — and that but in part — a single question: What, aside from genius, *made* the poet of the greater *Canterbury Tales*? How, in a word, did he master a technique at its height so consummate that it often seems not to be art at all, but the effortless play of nature? And by what various roads did he travel in passing from his earlier to his later themes? That twofold evolution, of technique and subject matter, is singularly rich in human as well as literary interest, and it is worth the effort to reconstruct, as far as possible, its processes.

One of the glories of English poetry has been the interpenetration in it of personal experience — call it for brevity life, if you will — and of books. Through the one, poetry acquires its stamp of individuality; through the other it is dipped in the quickening stream of tradition which has flowed through the work of all the poets from Homer and pre-Homeric days until now. The continuity of poetry, through its participation in that deep and perpetually broadening current, is a fact perhaps more important than the newness of the channels through which from time to time it flows. The greatest poetry is, indeed, steeped in the poet's own experience and coloured by the life of his times. But it also participates in a succession almost apostolic, in which there is an authentic if incorporeal laying on of hands:

> Go, litel book . . .
>   . . . no making thou n'envye,
> But subgit be to alle poesye;
> And kis the steppes, wher-as thou seest pace
> Virgile, Ovyde, Omer, Lucan, and Stace.

That is from the close of a masterpiece which is at once sheer Chaucer and an embodiment of the tradition of the elders from Homer through the Middle Ages to a contemporary fellow-poet, Boccaccio; and I suspect that no one in the long and splendid line of English poets more strikingly exemplifies than Geoffrey Chaucer the characteristic interplay, in great verse, of life and books. For he was, on the one hand, a widely experienced, busy, and versatile man of affairs, and he was also one of the most omnivorous readers in that company of glorious literary cormorants who have enriched English letters. Had he been either without the other — had there been lacking either the immediate and manifold contacts with life, or the zest of a *helluo librorum* — he would doubtless still have been a poet. But in that case not one of the poems by which he is known could even remotely have been what it is. Let me, then, rehearse as necessary background, even at the risk of seeming for the moment to abandon poetry, a few of the familiar facts.

No other English poet, in the first place, has approached Chaucer in the breadth and variety of his immediate, personal experience of life. For no other English poet — to pack a lifetime into a list — was a page in a royal household and for years Yeoman or Esquire at Court; was captured while in military service, and then ransomed by the King; was sent to Flanders, France, and Italy on half a dozen delicate and important diplomatic missions, involving royal marriages, commercial treaties, and treaties of peace; was Controller of the Customs and Subsidy of wools, hides, and wool-fells, and also Controller of Petty Customs, in the port of London; was Justice of the Peace, and member of Parliament; Clerk of the King's Works, with exacting duties and wide powers, at Westminster Palace, the Tower of London, the Castle of Berkhampstead, and at seven of the royal manors, with their gardens, mill-ponds, and fences; Surveyor, again with large authority, of walls, ditches, gutters, sewers, bridges, causeways, et cetera, along the Thames between Greenwich and Woolwich; Clerk of the Works at Windsor; Sub-Forester, and later Forester, in control of the great royal forest domain of Petherton in Somerset; and in the intervals holder of important wardships, and associated in the management of great estates.

And finally, not to omit the element of adventure, it may be doubted if there was ever another English poet who was twice robbed by highwaymen within three days. I have crammed into a catalogue, for the sake of their cumulative impact, the facts which everybody knows, but which we habitually contemplate piecemeal. And the active search still going on in the Records Office is bringing to light from time to time new items which further diversify the list. Had Chaucer never written a line of poetry, he would still have been known to his contemporaries as a trusted and capable public servant and a many-sided man of affairs.

What that rich experience meant for his art is for us the essential thing. But what it might have meant to it and by the grace of Heaven did not, it is neither irrelevant nor uninstructive to observe. Chaucer's French contemporary, Eustache Deschamps, who sent him a famous poetical epistle and who will meet us later, also led an active and a semi-public life, and into his twelve hundred *balades*, his one hundred and seventy-one *rondeaux*, his eighteen *virelais*, his fifteen *lais*, which nobody ever reads any more except as documents, he poured on occasion the minute and personal details of his variegated career — dates and places meticulously noted; incidents of his campaigns in Flanders; the racy interchange of bilingual amenities with two Englishmen as he and Othon de Graunson (Chaucer's 'flour of hem that make in Fraunce') one day rode through Calais; the fleas at the inn that night; his personal ailments; his distaste for tripe and truffles. Now Chaucer had at his fingers' ends more such themes for verse than ever Deschamps dreamed. Read sometime, for its equally sinister possibilities, the inventory in the *Life Records* which Chaucer turned in when he resigned the Clerkship of the Works — pages on pages of rakes, ladles, crowbars, hurdles for scaffolds — one remembers how 'joly Absalon,' the parish clerk, played Herod 'on a scaffold hye' — andirons innumerable, a broken cable ('frangitur et devastatur'), images made in the likeness of kings, '100 round stones called engynstones,' bottles, buckets, and (from the Tower of London of all places) a frying-pan. And there were also the sewers and the gutters and the ditches. What use Deschamps would have made of such opportunities does not admit of contemplation. But only once that I can recall in the whole wide range of his poetry does Chaucer give even a hint of his participation in affairs. It was in another and a different fashion that his extraordinarily varied experience played into the hands of his art. And if in what follows I may seem for a time to have wholly forgotten that art, I can only ask you to believe that I have not.

What that experience gave to Chaucer was, of course, first of all an opportunity almost unrivalled for wide and intimate knowledge of almost every sort of actor in the human comedy. We are apt to forget in thinking of him the remarkable range of his acquaintance with men and women in virtually

every station, rank, and occupation of the diversified
society in which he lived. He was a member of the
household, first of a prince of the blood and then of
a king, and through his marriage belonged to the
circle of John of Gaunt and Henry of Derby. He
counted among his acquaintances and friends great
nobles and knights who had travelled far, and fought
in all quarters of the known world. On his missions
abroad he was associated with men of wide experience and influence in State affairs; met in France
and Flanders statesmen versed in diplomacy; and
matched his wits in Italy with Bernabò Visconti —
'God of delyt, and scourge of Lumbardye,' as he
called him when the message reached him of his
sudden end. The very first record that we have of
him contains a reference to a visit of Prince Lionel
and the Countess of Ulster, on whom he was then
in attendance, to the Benedictine Nunnery of Saint
Leonards, at the Prioress's Stratford atte Bowe, and
from then to the close of his life he had intimate
knowledge in a score of ways — through members of
his own family, connexions by marriage, and the
infinite ramifications of the Church's influence upon
affairs — of ecclesiastics of every feather. With men
of law he came, through various exigencies, into
close relations, and there is reason to think that he
may himself have been a member of Lincoln's Inn.
He had business dealings for years with merchants
and shipmen, and through his Clerkships of the
Works and his Surveyorships, with masons and car-
penters and hedgers and ditchers and unskilled

labour of every sort. And how close his relations with the tradesmen and the craftsmen of the guilds were bound up with his own political career, Professor Kuhl years ago made clear. Now and then one gets a glimpse of that rare and precious thing a concrete incident, as when one sees him (in that record which Miss Rickert turned up a year or so ago) going down from the Customs to Dartmouth about a Genoese tarit, the 'Saint Mary and Saint George' — its master one Johannes de Nigris of Genoa — which had been driven ashore on the coast of Brittany, and which John Hawley, then Mayor of Dartmouth, was charged with robbing. And one of Hawley's ships was called the 'Maudelayne,' and Chaucer had the trick of turning official business to good poetic account. There are still vast uncharted regions of the Public Records to explore, but Professor Manly's recent studies of them have given as never before — whether or not we grant this or that tentative conclusion — flesh and blood and sometimes local habitation to the sergeants of law, the merchants, franklins and shipmen, the millers and weavers, the archdeacons, canons, summoners, friars, pardoners, prioresses and nuns, whom Chaucer first knew for his day and then bequeathed to eternity.

But this wide range of his experience carries with it another consequence. We need constantly to remind ourselves of the degree to which in Chaucer's day communication had to be by word of mouth. And so the people whom he knew were also chan-

nels through which came to him news of his world
— news not only of that 'little world' which to
Shakespeare's John of Gaunt was England; not
only, either, of that 'queasy world' (in Margaret
Paston's vivid phrase) across the Channel; but also
of that now looming, menacing, always mysterious
world beyond, which was the Orient. And few
men have ever been more strategically placed for its
reception. That news of England or Wales or even
Ireland should so reach him is too obvious to dwell
on, fascinating as is the use he makes of it. How,
for example, did he get to know of that 'Colle
tregetour' — Colin the magician — whom he saw
in his dream in the House of Fame?

> Ther saugh I Colle tregetour
> Upon a table of sicamour
> Pleye an uncouthe thing to telle;
> I saugh him carien a wind-melle
> Under a walsh-note shelle.

But Colle was actually no piquant figure in a dream.
He was, as we now know, thanks to Professor
Royster, a contemporary Englishman, and he later
exhibited his tricks, 'par voie de nigromancie,' at
Orleans, precisely as the Clerk of Orleans in the
Franklin's Tale produced his illusions, 'Swiche as
thise subtile tregetoures playe.' And Chaucer's
apposite choice of Orleans as the school of his own
magician is not without interest. How, too (to draw
on the House of Fame again), did he get to know of
Bret Glascurion and of Celtic wicker houses? Did
that Welsh vintner of London tell him — Lewis

Johan, who was at least a friend of Chaucer once removed; or did Sir Lewis Clifford or Sir John Clanvowe, both close friends of his, and both of whom held offices in Wales? Who can say! Chaucer's London was his own vast House of Rumour, only on a smaller scale.

But men, among them scores whom Chaucer knew, were constantly going out of England and coming back to it — going out for reasons of war, or trade, or chivalry, or religion, and coming back along the trade routes and the pilgrim roads' and from their military exploits, with stories, and tidings, and even manuscripts, as well as with stuffs, or spices, or cockle-shells, or battered arms. And such knights as the stately figure of the Prologue were among the great intermediaries between Chaucer's England and the rest of the world. Europe was being menaced from three directions at once. We sometimes forget that Tamerlane's life just overlapped Chaucer's at each end, and that it was in the year in which Chaucer was appointed Justice of the Peace that the Great Turk boasted that he would make his horse eat oats on the high altar of St. Peter's. And Chaucer's Knight had fought in Europe, Asia, and Africa against the Moors, the Turks, the Tartars and the heathen of the North — in Turkey, Spain, Prussia, Lithuania (then a Tartar outpost) and Russia, and also with 'that valorous champion of impossible conquests,' Pierre de Lusignan, King of Cyprus, at the taking of Alexandria, and at Lyeys and Satalye. And the knight was a composite portrait of men whom Chaucer personally knew. Of the witnesses (to give a single instance) who testified with Chaucer in the Scrope-Grosvenor case, Nicholas Sambraham, Esquire, had seen Sir Stephen Scrope at the taking of Alexandria, and in Hungary, Prussia, and Constantinople, and had seen Sir Henry Scrope in Spain, and, as he says, 'beyond the great sea in many places and in many chivalrous exploits.' Sir Richard Waldegrave had seen Sir William Scrope with the King of Cyprus at Satalye in Turkey; and Sir Henry de Ferrers and John de Rither, Esquire, had seen Sir Geoffrey Scrope in Prussia and Lithuania. And these half-dozen names we know through the accident of a dispute about the bearing of certain arms. There are more, but these are enough to show that the campaigns of Chaucer's Knight were the campaigns of Chaucer's acquaintances and friends. And they, like the Knight, had been associated with fellow knights of all the other nations which, with England, were making common cause against a common foe. And such stories as circulated about those Tables of Honour, like that at the head of which the Knight had often sat 'aboven alle naciouns in Pruce,' and tales of that gallant and meteoric figure, the King of Cyprus, whose death Chaucer bewailed 'in maner of Tragedie,' and of tournaments at Tramissene and sea-fights off the coasts of Africa and Asia Minor — such stories a score of Chaucer's friends could tell. For warfare was a more leisured business then than now — witness the Barbary expedition, of which Chaucer's friends Sir Lewis Clifford and Sir John Clanvowe were members, during which war-like expedition the gay and amorous *Cent Balades* were composed. And finally — to come closer home — it was to a meeting in France, during a pause in the Hundred Years' War, between this same friend Sir Lewis Clifford and Eustache Deschamps, that there came to Chaucer the manuscript which sug-gested his best-known passage outside the Canter-bury Tales; as it was through a later meeting be-tween the same two men, during the negotiations for a truce, that Chaucer received another manu-script which gave him rich material for the most famous portrait in the Tales themselves.

Chivalry, too, played its curious part. Don Quixote, Professor Ker once observed with chapter and verse, would have been perfectly at home with the Knights and Squires of Chaucer's day, and would not have been thought extravagant in either principles or practice. And with that dictum no student of the period will disagree. And so young Squires who, like Machaut's and Chaucer's, bore them well in arms 'in hope to stonden in [hir] lady grace,' were still being sent by their ladies to win further grace, 'in-to Walakye, To Pruyse and in-to Tartarye, To Alisaundre, ne in-to Turkye,' and finally charged, for the crowning exploit, to 'Go hoodles to the drye see, And come hoom by the Carrenar.' And that last injunction is a singularly apposite case in point. For we now know, as Sir Aurel Stein's latest maps and photographs at last unmistakably show, that an actual Kara-nor, or Black Lake, lies a short stone's throw from Marco Polo's highway, in the heart of Central Asia, beyond the dry, salt-incrusted bed of an ancient inland sea. And through some merchant or other this bit of flotsam and jetsam had probably drifted back along the silk routes, perhaps through Lyeys, where the Knight had fought, along with who can tell what tales of Tartary, such as that which the Squire himself was to rehearse.

For merchants, with pilgrims and shipmen, were also recognized bearers of news, and as such Chaucer, on whose own testimony I am drawing, knew them well. 'Ye ben fadres of tydinges And tales,' exclaims the Man of Law in his apostrophe to merchants; 'Tydings of sondry regnes' he goes on, and of 'the wondres that they mighte seen or here.' And it was a merchant, he declares, who years ago told him the very tale he tells — a story which begins in Syria and wanders by way of the Pillars of Hercules to England, and back by the strait to Italy. For England, like all of Europe, was full of tales — tales which through centuries had travelled by mysterious routes from Arabia and Hindostan and Burma and Tibet and Turkey and Siberia — narratives ageless and timeless, with no abiding place; rubbed smooth in their endless passings, like pebbles rounded by the waves, or Chinese carvings polished by uncounted generations of hands. Nor was it only merchants along the trade routes who were their vehicles. Chaucer's House of Rumour

'Was ful of shipmen and pilgrymes, With scrippes bret-ful of lesinges, Entremedled with tydinges.' And pilgrims like that notable wayfarer the Wife of Bath, who had thrice been at Jerusalem, and 'had passed many a straunge streem,' were visiting 'ferne halwes, couthe in sondry londes,' and coming back, like the merchants, with multifarious information, false and true. It was along the pilgrim roads, as we now well know, that the stories of Charlemagne and Roland and the twelve peers of France passed over the Alps into Italy. And pilgrims told their tales, and Chaucer was a marvellous listener. His Dartmouth shipman, too, whose own harbour was one of the English ports for ships from the Orient, knew 'alle the havenes, as they were, From Gootlond to the cape of Finistere, And every cryke in Britayne and in Spayne.' And Gothland, with the other havens at which he and his fellows touched, was connected through the Hanseatic trade with Novgorod, and Novgorod, like the ports in Asia Minor where Chaucer's friends had fought, had been for hundreds of years a terminus of those ancient Eastern trade-routes along which had travelled, with the merchants and the shipmen, tales like those which underlie the *fabliaux* and a dozen of the stories which the Canterbury pilgrims tell. And Chaucer sat at the receipt of custom in the port of London, 'at the quay called Woolwharf in the Tower Ward.' And the man who, between nightfall and bedtime, had spoken with every one of the nine and twenty pilgrims at the Tabard

Inn was not the man to refrain from incidental conversation with the mariners whose lawful occasions brought them to his quay.

How this or that particular tale or bit of information came to Chaucer, it is far from my present purpose to inquire. He was at the centre of a rich and varied and shifting world, and in ways without number, of which these are bare suggestions, his personal and official experience lent material to his art. And there were also books.

The range of Chaucer's reading is as extraordinary as the scope of his activities. He read in three languages besides English — French, Latin, and Italian. French he probably both knew and spoke from his childhood. Latin with little doubt he learned at school. It has hitherto been assumed that he picked up Italian in Italy, during his first visit in 1372–73. It is possible, though not yet proven, that he may have known it earlier. But in either case, the bulk of his known reading, until the great Italians swam into his ken, was French, with a good deal of Latin besides. And French he never abandoned, and Latin he read copiously to the end. The French and Italian works which he knew may best for our purpose be considered later. His wide and diversified reading of Latin, however, is both typical of his varied interests and important for its contributions, and I shall rapidly summarize it here.

Of the classics he knew in the original Ovid, especially the *Metamorphoses* (his 'owne book,' as he called it), and the *Heroides*. Virgil he knew, but apparently only the *Aeneid*; the *Thebaid* of Statius; Claudian; and either in Latin or French or both, the *Pharsalia*. Cicero's *Somnium Scipionis* he read in a copy of the commentary of Macrobius which he or somebody else had thumbed to pieces — 'myn olde book to-torn,' as he refers to it. Horace he quotes half a dozen times, but I doubt whether he knew either Horace or Juvenal at first hand. Dante, or John of Salisbury, or the *florilegia* may well have been intermediaries. But for Virgil, Statius, and Lucan, and also for Ovid, he had two strings to his bow. For the Middle Ages seized upon the Latin epics and made them over into their own likeness as romances. And so there was, for the *Aeneid*, the *Roman d'Eneas*, in which both Dido and (especially) Lavinia sigh, wake, and 'walwe,' like Chaucer's own Dido in the *Legend*, in the throes of heroic love. For the *Thebaid*, too, there was the *Roman de Thèbes*, and for the *Pharsalia* the *Roman de Julius Cesar*. And the Homeric story of the Trojan War passed by devious ways into the *Roman de Troie* of Benoit de St^e-Maure, and thence to Guido delle Colonne. The *Metamorphoses* were transmogrified into the interminable and portentous triple allegory of the *Ovide moralisé*, on which Machaut had freely drawn for his classical lore. They are all, as I can testify, diverting documents, after their fantastic fashion, even yet, and Chaucer, who probably in his salad days read French more readily than Latin, and who also would be apt to read what his fellow

pages and squires at Court were reading, certainly
knew and freely used the *Roman de Troie*, and drew,
on occasion, upon the *Ovide moralisé*. He also read
— I feel sure myself on grounds which have no
place here — the *Roman d'Eneas* and the *Roman de
Julius Cesar*. And there is evidence that he knew the
mythographers, and was not unfamiliar with the
mass of misinformation accumulated in the medieval
commentaries on the classics. It was, in fact, more
than once Servius or Lactantius or Junius Philar-
gerius who either directly or indirectly first made
for him his mistakes. For few things about Chaucer
are more important to remember than the fact
that even the classical authors whom he read in the
original were deeply coloured in his mind through
the various medieval metamorphoses which they
had undergone.

His reading in the medieval Latin authors was
far too extensive for enumeration here. But nothing
in his dealings with them is more characteristic
than his trick of suffusing with his own inalienable
humour his borrowings from the dullest and most
arid documents. He knew well both the *Anticlau-
dianus* and the *De Planctu Naturae* of Alanus de
Insulis, and especially remembered, as he would,
the concrete bits, and enriched them, as he also
would, with an added liveliness. He read Martianus
Capella on the Nuptials of Philology and Mercury,
and Nigel Wireker's diverting Mirror of Fools, with
the adventures of Dan Burnel the ass; and a scrap
of the Eclogue of Theodulus once leaped back to

his memory, endowed with an exquisite humour which he did not find in his original. He knew, as a student of his art who did not 'pipe but as the linnets sing,' the *Nova Poetria* of Geoffrey of Vinsauf, whom he calls his 'dere mayster soverayn,' and he made irresistible mock-heroic use, in the Nun's Priest's Tale, of one of his master's *exempla*. He at least dipped into the vast encyclopedic reaches of Vincent of Beauvais, and he read with obvious gusto and astounding results Saint Jerome's tractate against Jovinian on the subject of virginity. He was thoroughly familiar (to shift the key) with the Vulgate, and with the service and especially the great hymns of the Church, which inspired — in each case interwoven with lines from the crowning vision of the *Paradiso* — at least two of his loftiest passages. Whether he saw as he read the rich potentialities of his documents, or whether his stores came pouring back to memory as he composed, or whether both processes went on together, we can never know. But if anyone ever read (in the current phrase) 'creatively,' it was he.

And to all this evidence of abounding vitality and energy must be added the almost incredible list of his translations. The refrain of the *Balade* which Eustache Deschamps addressed to Chaucer and sent by the hand of Sir Lewis Clifford, is the line: 'Grant translateur, noble Geffroy Chaucier.' It was as a translator only, it would seem, that his fame had reached Deschamps. And the *Balade* itself makes it clear that Deschamps had in mind that translation of the *Roman de la Rose* which, in the Prologue to the *Legend*, gave such offence to the God of Love. And the God of Love's anger makes it further clear that Jean de Meun's huge continuation was included. As if this great task were not enough, he translated Jean de Meun's French version of Albertano of Brescia's *Liber Consolationis*, and also (for his tastes were richly catholic) the fierce misanthropy of Pope Innocent's *De Contemptu Mundi*, at which gloomy treatise Deschamps too had tried his hand. And there were besides the now lost translations of a work of Origen on Mary Magdalene, and of Machaut's *Dit dou Lyon*. But above all the rest stands Boethius *On the Consolation of Philosophy*. He translated it, as Alfred the Great and Jean de Meun had done before him, and with the aid of Jean de Meun's French version, and he drew upon it, as in another fashion he levied tribute on the *Roman de la Rose*, until he ceased to write.

His reading in the science of his day is in some respects, I am inclined to think, the most remarkable of all. His singularly broad yet minute knowledge of medieval medicine, in which he anticipated Burton, I have elsewhere had occasion to discuss. But far more than his acquaintance with 'the loveres maladye of Hereos' is in point. Fourteenth-century medicine, like its twentieth-century descendant, was half psychology, and in its emphasis on dreams as a means of diagnosis anticipated Freud. And Madame Pertelote's diagnosis, by means of his dream, of Chauntecleer's malady, as well as her inimitable discourse on dreams as symptoms, is scientifically accurate. So is her *materia medica*. The herbs which she prescribes — 'Pekke hem up right as they growe, and ete hem in' — are the medically proper herbs. And the quintessential touch is her inclusion in Chauntecleer's dietary of 'wormes' for 'a day or two.' For worms — you may read a learned and matter-of-fact chapter on *Vermes ter-renae* in the *Medica Materia* of Dioscorides — were among the recognized correctives. It is easy enough to slip into one's narrative as evidence of erudition an excerpt from some learned document. But such casual exactness, imbued with delicious humour to boot, is not something which one gets up over night. In alchemy — witness the Canon's Yeoman's Tale — Chaucer was no less deeply grounded than in medicine. He had read enough in the alchemical treatises of Arnoldus de Villanova, for example, his 'Arnold of the Newe Toun,' to ascribe to one of Arnold's treatises a highly picturesque and abstruse dictum which he quotes, when he had actually read it in another. As for physics, one of the very best pieces of exposition, as exposition, which I know in English is the erudite Eagle's discourse in the House of Fame on the transmission of sound, and that again is founded on accepted authority. So is Chaucer's astrology, and in astronomy proper he could point with just pride to that Treatise on the Astrolabe which he wrote, with its charming Pre-face, for his 'litel son Lowis,' using freely a Latin translation of the Arabian astronomer Messahala. These are the barest shreds and patches only. The scope and thoroughness of Chaucer's scientific reading would still be remarkable, had he read nothing else.

There, then, are the raw materials of his art — men and their doings, and books — God's plenty of each, in all conscience. And since he began with books (with which, to be sure, he never ended) it is much to the point to consider how he read. Did he have the books on our list, for example, in his own possession, and therefore ready at hand for pleasure or need?

Without question a large, perhaps a very large proportion of them were his own. He declared, fairly late in his life — or rather, the God of Love asserted for him — that he had in his chest 'sixty bokes, olde and newe,' and there is no reason to doubt the statement. But that number may easily have represented three or four times sixty 'books,' in the sense in which we use the word. For book, as Chaucer employs the term, must be thought of in the light of medieval manuscripts, and a single manuscript was often a small library in itself. The 'boke' which Chaucer was reading when he fell asleep over the tale of Ceyx and Alcyone was an omnium gatherum of verse, and lives of queens and kings, and 'many othere thinges smale.' The 'book' (and again the word is the same) which the Wife of Bath's fifth husband revelled in contained, she declared, Valerius *ad Rufinum*, Theophrastus,

Jerome against Jovinian, Tertullian, the mysterious Crisippus, Trotula, the Epistles of Eloise, the Parables of Solomon, and the *Ars Amatoria* — 'And alle thise were bounden in o volume.' And one need only recall, among extant examples, the Auchinleck MS., with its more than forty separate pieces, or, for that matter, Harley 7333 among the manuscripts of the Canterbury Tales. Chaucer's library was a rich one for his day, and like his own clerk of Oxford who had 'at his beddes heed' his 'Twenty bokes, clad in blak or reed,' and like that clerk of another kidney, 'hende Nicholas,' who likewise kept in his lodgings 'his Almageste, and bokes grete and smale . . . On shelves couched at his beddes heed,' one may be fairly sure that Chaucer's sixty books were not far from his hand.

But is there any way of knowing, aside from these more or less material considerations, how he actually read? There are two subjects, and two only, on which Chaucer vouchsafes us personal information about himself — his love of books, and his imperviousness, real or assumed, to love. On those two topics he is, in William Wordsworth's phrase but with a difference, 'right voluble.' And two passages are especially in point. In one, that preternaturally intelligent bird, the Eagle of the House of Fame, gently chides him for his habits. He knows nothing now, says the Eagle, of what is going on about him; even 'of thy verray neyghebores That dwellen almost at thy dores, Thou herest neither that ne this.' And then follows, under cover of the Eagle's irre-

sponsible loquacity, the most precious autobiographical touch that Chaucer left:

> For whan thy labour doon al is,
> And hast y-maad thy rekeninges,
> In stede of reste and newe thinges,
> Thou gost hoom to thy hous anoon;
> And, also domb as any stoon,
> Thou sittest at another boke,
> Til fully daswed is thy loke,
> And livest thus as an hermyte,
> Although thyn abstinence is lyte.

That picture — the account books of the customs
exchanged after hours for vastly different books (the
Eagle's 'another' is pregnant), and Chaucer reading
on, oblivious of all else, until his eyes dazzle in his
head — that picture tells more than pages, not
merely of the intimate relation in which his books
stood to his business, but also of the absorbed intentness with which he read.   And there is another passage which illuminates yet another quality of his
reading. 'Not yore agon,' he writes in the **Parlement of Foules**,

> ... hit happed me for to beholde
> Upon a boke, was write with lettres olde;
> And ther-upon, *a certeyn thing to lerne*,
> The longe day *ful faste I radde and yerne*.

I do not know which is the more characteristic of
Chaucer — the fact that he was reading with the
definite purpose of learning a certain thing, or the
fact that he was reading fast and eagerly. The two
belong together. You cannot divide his invincible

zest from his incorrigibly inquiring spirit — that 'besy gost' of his, as he called it once, 'that thrusteth alwey newe.' And because he brought both to his books, his reading became a live and plastic thing for his art to seize on.

He was gifted, finally, with another quality of mind which is peculiarly bound up with his art. He possessed, in a word, like Virgil and Milton and Coleridge, a powerfully associative memory, which played, as he read, over the multitude of impressions from previous reading, with which his mind was stored. And the zest with which he read gave freshness to his recollections, and one can sometimes almost see the hovering associations precipitate themselves as he reads. A single phrase in Boccaccio (and I am speaking by the book) calls up the lines of a famous passage in Dante in which the same phrase occurs, and the result is a *tertium quid* of his own, enriched from the spoils of both. He finds in Boccaccio's *Filostrato*, as he works it over into his own Troilus, the lovely Virgilian simile of the lily cut by the plough and withering. But Dante, in a canto of the *Inferno*, the opening lines of which Chaucer elsewhere quotes, has a simile of falling, withering leaves. And again, through a common element, Boccaccio's lines recall the lines of Dante, and the falling leaves replace the fading lily in Chaucer's simile. And Boccaccio and Dante in turn had each in like fashion recalled his simile from Virgil. It would be easy to rehearse such instances by the score — instances, too, in which with his reminiscences of books are interwoven his recollections of experience. For that continuity of poetry of which I spoke consists in the perpetual enrichment, through just such incremental transformations, of the present through the past. And one of the happiest gifts of the gods to English poetry, at the strategic moment of its history, was that prehensile, amalgamating memory of Chaucer's which had for its playground the prodigious array of promiscuous writings which a moment ago I ruthlessly catalogued.

What now of his art in its larger relations? For everything that I have so far said has been said with that definitely in view. It is perilous, in the first place, to divide Chaucer's poetic biography mechanically into periods. There was nothing cataclysmic about his development. He was not a new creature, as Professor Kittredge once observed, when he came back to London from his first visit to Italy, nor does the poet of the Canterbury Tales startle us by a 'leap of buds into ripe flowers.' Rather — if I too may yield to an association — 'Morn into noon did pass, noon into eve.' Transitions there were, of course, but they were gradual. French poetry yielded first place to Italian, and both to an absorption in human life, in which books and men were fused as in a crucible. But even after his momentous discovery of Boccaccio and Dante, the influence of French poetry went on, though its character changed — changed (to put it briefly) from the mood of Guillaume de Lorris and Machaut to the mood of Jean de Meun and Deschamps and the *fabliaux*. And *pari passu*, as his powers developed, there came a significant shift of values, and his reading of books played a lesser and his reading of life a larger rôle in his art. But throughout his career, that art kept curiously even pace with his active life. It was dominantly French while he was in personal attendance on a court where French was still the more familiar language. His so-called Italian period, which was never Italian in the sense in which the earlier period had been French, coincided roughly with those activities — his missions and the customs — which brought him into various relations with Italy, Italians, and Italian letters. And when his broadening affairs afforded wider opportunities for observation, his art, keeping all that it had won from France and Italy, became at once English and universal.

Everybody knows that Chaucer began as a follower of the contemporary French school of poetry, and that the most powerful influence upon that school was the thirteenth-century *Roman de la Rose*. But the *Roman de la Rose* was influential in two entirely different ways. Guillaume de Lorris, who began it, was a dreamer of dreams and a poet of exquisite grace and charm. Jean de Meun, who continued it and multiplied its length by five, was a caustic and disillusioned satirist, trenchant, arrogant, and absolute master of a mordant pen. If Pope had taken it into his head to complete the *Faerie Queene*, or if Swift had been seized by the fancy of carrying on the *Rape of the Lock* in the mood of Gulliver's fierce misanthropy, we might have had an adequate parallel. And the fourteenth-century French poets, as a consequence of this strange duplex authorship, fall roughly into two schools — the sons of Guillaume de Lorris and the sons of Jean de Meun. But common to them all, and giving the framework to half their verse, was the allegorical love vision.

The contemporary Frenchmen whose influence on Chaucer was farthest reaching were three: Guillaume de Machaut, an elder contemporary; Jean Froissart, his coeval; and Eustache Deschamps, who was younger. Machaut, who like Chaucer was courtier and man of affairs as well as poet, and who with his master, John of Bohemia, had 'reysed,' like the Knight, against the 'mescreans' in Prussia and the Tartars in the snows of Lithuania, was the most influential French poet of his day. And he was so chiefly by virtue of a highly sophisticated, artificial, exquisitely elaborated technique. Froissart, whom Chaucer probably knew at Court as the protégé of Queen Philippa, was an incomparably less finished craftsman than Machaut, to whose school he belongs. When he tells a story, like that in the *Dit dou Florin*, of his reading aloud to Gaston Phebus, Count of Foix, night after night for weeks, his interminable *Méliador*, the tale becomes, through the art of the chronicler, vivid with firelight and candles and flagons; and when he writes of his boyhood and young manhood — of the games that he played, and of the maiden whom he one day found reading the *Cléomadès* — his verse is suffused with personal charm. But when he falls into the vein of the school, he can be both long-winded and very dull. And finally Deschamps, who calls Machaut his master, but who was really of the tribe of Jean de Meun, was an inordinately prolific versifier, with the skill of a virtuoso, but without music, grace, or charm; could be as minutely circumstantial as Mistress Quickly over her silver-gilt goblet; and was possessed by a passion like that of Pepys for autobiographical memoranda. Of the three, Machaut was Chaucer's earliest master; from Froissart he effectively borrowed more than once; and Deschamps twice furnished him with subject matter to which, on the two occasions, each time with a technique already mastered, he gave consummate form. There were others, of course, but these three were the chief influences during the period when Chaucer was saturated with the later French poetry of courtly love, even while maintaining an amiable impermeability all his own to its inherent absurdities. And I am far from sure that it was not to these very absurdities that Chaucer's genius owed the turn which from the first it took.

For he found in his French models, and especially in Machaut, the framework of the vision, as that had come down, with growing elaboration on the way, from Guillaume de Lorris. And he used the machinery of the vision in the Book of the Duchess, the House of Fame, the Parliament of Fowls, and in the first version of the Prologue to the Legend of Good Women. It was the most popular and, in Machaut's expert hands, the most sophisticated device of his day, and Chaucer was then writing for a sophisticated audience. But the visions were allegorical love visions, and as such they were thick sown with artifices at which Chaucer balked. And the more thoroughly one is steeped in Chaucer, so that one sees in a measure with his eyes, the more readily one understands the impossibility of his acquiescence in the then current artificialities of the *genre*. The framework of the vision, to be sure, offered freedom in both choice and disposition of subject matter. But it was precisely in the character of the French subject matter, to judge from the cold shoulder which Chaucer turned to it, that one source of his disrelish lay. For it was obviously as barren of interest to Geoffrey Chaucer as interminable subtilizings about love — especially when nothing comes of them — have been and are to any normally constituted Anglo-Saxon. Moreover, the visions are thickly peopled with personified abstractions. Esperance, Attemprance, Mesure, Douce Pensée, Plaisance, Desirs, Franchise, Pité, Loyauté, Espoirs, Raison, Suffisance, Patience, Paour — those are the denizens of less than half of Machaut's *Remede de Fortune*. Like Criseyde listening under trying circumstances to the 'wommanisshe thinges' of her feminine callers, Chaucer must have 'felte almost [his] herte dye For wo, and wery of that companye.' Nor was it subject matter alone which he found alien. The phraseology, too, was remote alike from his tastes and his aptitudes. There is nothing I know which rivals in its tireless facility of recurrence the later vocabulary of courtly love. If one read long enough, one is obsessed by the uncanny feeling that the phraseology walks alone, without need of the poet's intervention, and carries the poet with it of its own momentum. Specific meaning disappears. Machaut's Peronne, in that amazing Goethe-and-Bettina correspondence, the *Voir-Dit*, is 'en douceur douce com coulombelle, En loyauté loyal com turturelle.' But the same columbine phrases slip from his pen, when, in *Prise d'Alexandrie*, he describes the Emperor Charles I of Luxembourg. He too, like Peronne, is 'humbles et piteus Plus que turtre ne colombele.' In that ineffably affected jargon discriminations vanish. 'Thought and affliction, passion, hell itself, [are turned] to favour and to prettiness.' And that was not Chaucer's way.

What he found, then, in the French vision poems, was a *frame* — a frame which possessed admirable potentialities, but which for him, to all intents and purposes, was empty. And Chaucer, who in his way was not unlike Nature herself, abhorred a vacuum. He proceeded, accordingly, to fill the frame, and incidentally to set one of the great traditions of English poetry. And into the vision framework, instead of consecrated phrases, wire drawn subtleties, *ragionamente d'amore*, and the more fantastic elements of the courtly code, he poured

the stores of that reading and observation on which
we have dwelt so long. 'For out of olde feldes' —
and this was his discovery, as 'the longe day ful
faste [he] radde and yerne' —

> For out of olde feldes, as man seith,
> Cometh al this newe corn fro yeer to yere;
> And out of olde bokes, in good feith,
> Cometh al this newe science that men lere.

And into the old bottles Chaucer poured with lav-
ish hand a new and heady wine.

What happened may best be seen by a glance at
his first three vision poems. His earliest essay, the
Book of the Duchess, was made before he went to
Italy, when his reading was almost wholly French,
and when Machaut in particular was at his finger
tips. It is a vision poem, with all the paraphernalia
of the *genre*, and it is also an elegy — an elegy on the
death of the Duchess Blanche, the first wife of his
patron, John of Gaunt. But into the conventional
frame he fits, with tact and feeling, and with conspicuous skill in adapting them to his ends, materials
drawn from what was then his reading — to wit, in
this instance, from no less than eight of Machaut's
poems and one (at least) of Froissart's. Save for
scattered reminiscences of the Bible, the *Roman de la
Rose*, Boethius, and Benoit, there is little else. His
instinct from the beginning was to enrich, and those
were the stores which he then possessed. But his
borrowings are interwoven with such art that for
more than five hundred years nobody suspected

that the poem was not all of a piece. And even
when his appropriations are most unmistakable,
they are still miraculously Chaucer and not Machaut. The little whelp that came creeping up, as
if it knew him, to the Dreamer, and 'Hild doun his
heed and joyned his eres, And leyde al smothe doun
his heres' — that bewitching English puppy is
Chaucer's metamorphosis of a fantastic lion, which
Carpaccio would have revelled in, native to the
bizarre landscape of the *Dit dou Lyon* of Machaut.
And into his version of Machaut's catalogue of those
remote regions to which the courtly lovers were dis-
patched to win their spurs, Chaucer has slipped that
precious bit of hearsay about the Dry Sea and the
Carrenar. The Book of the Duchess is not a masterpiece, but it is significant far beyond its intrinsic
merit. For in it for the first time, with the still
limited resources at his command, Chaucer loaded
every rift with ore. And now the ore grew steadily
richer.

For Chaucer went to Italy, and learned to read
Boccaccio and Dante, and all the while that knowledge of books and men on which we have dwelt
was broadening and deepening. The French influence waned as that of Italy waxed, but the shift
of emphasis was gradual, and the vision poems still
went on. And into the three that followed the Book
of the Duchess poured those steadily growing stores.
He begins the House of Fame — to follow what
seems to me to be the true succession — a little
dully, with a long résumé of the *Aeneid,* and an inter-

lude from the *Metamorphoses*. And both the *Roman d'Eneas* and the *Ovide moralisé* were summoned, I feel certain, to his aid. Then all at once, into a desert recalled from Lucan sweeps an eagle which owed its sunlike brightness to the *Paradiso*, and the poem becomes vivid with new life. And the significant thing is not so much that the amazing eagle, throughout the flight through the air, shows himself equally at home in Ovid, and Boethius, and Theodulus, and Macrobius, and Dante's *Convito* and can even recognize Chaucer's unspoken thoughts of Martianus Capella and Alanus, as that he is a new and unique creation — as much a person as his creator, and utterly unthinkable in any vision which Machaut and his fellows ever dreamed. And only the keenest observer of men, endowed with the rarest humour, could have conceived the inimitable conversation which goes on, as the little earth recedes to a speck and the signs of the zodiac are left behind; and the poet of the Canterbury Tales is already present in that immortal dialogue. Then, into the third book, ushered in, like the second, by an invocation drawn from Dante, pours a phantasmagoria which Rabelais might have envied, and which defies all summary — reminiscences of books treading on the heels of recollections of experience, in bewildering profusion. Within the compass of thirty-five lines — to take a relatively simple passage only — Chaucer's memory, as the verse flows on without a ripple, has flashed to Boethius, and the *Roman de la Rose*, and a line from the *Metamorphoses*, and some account or other which he had read in the romances of those whirling houses which were a peculiarly captivating item in the romantic stock-in-trade, and Celtic wicker houses which he had either seen himself or heard of from his friends, and the noise of 'engynstones' remembered from his own campaign in France. Sketched as I am sketching it, the poem is a thing of shreds and patches. It is not so on the page. But I am putting asunder what Chaucer joined together, in order to give the barest inkling of the thronging recollections which, in his vision poems, his art curbed and concealed.

And now, in the Parlement of Foules, France slips gradually into the background and Italy assumes the major rôle. The cadre of the vision is still retained, but the familiar French couplet is discarded, and rime royal takes its place. In the last two books of the House of Fame Chaucer's crowding recollections are swept along as by a torrent; in the close-packed introductory sections of the Parlement there is a new serenity, and a sense of beauty which has been quickened and deepened alike. For the influence of Dante and Boccaccio upon Chaucer is to be sought not merely or even chiefly in his borrowings and imitations, but rather through the impregnation of his art with qualities which his earlier French masters never knew. And in the first half of the Parlement Chaucer's memory is busy with the Divine Comedy, and both his memory and his eyes with the *Teseide*. The

Proem opens with a rendering, in a master's hand, of the first axiom of Hippocrates —

> The lyf so short, the craft so long to lerne,
> Th' assay so hard, so sharp the conquering.

It was a favourite with those elder medical authorities whom Chaucer read, and I suspect it came from them. Then, passing to the book which he had just been reading 'faste and yerne' all day long, he gives (I am sure for his own delight) a summary — compact and lucid and urbane — of the *Somnium Scipionis*. And night falls in the words with which Dante describes the first fall of evening in the *Inferno*. Then Chaucer's unrest before he sleeps recalls Boethius, and the thought of dreams brings back to mind the famous lines of Claudian, and because (as Chaucer shrewdly suggests) he has just been reading the dream of Scipio, Scipio himself becomes his guide. And the Proem ends with a flash of memory back to Jean de Meun.

Of the next one hundred lines or so, Boccaccio's *Teseide*, through a score of its most graphic and beautiful stanzas, has the lion's share. Twice at least, too, a phrase of Boccaccio recalls a passage of Dante, and the *Divina Commedia* and the *Teseide* flow together into a mould which is Chaucer's own. And *Inferno*, *Purgatorio*, and *Paradiso* are now all three at command. Then all at once the whole character of the vision changes. From the robe of the 'noble emperesse' Nature in Aleyn's 'Pleynt of Kinde,' Chaucer sweeps the birds of the air, which

Alanus had depicted on it, adds others of his own, and sets them down before Nature, alive and gifted with the power of speech, in parliament assembled. And whatever, if any, the ulterior purpose of the poem, that assembly, with its unerring adjustment of sentiments and language to the ranks and classes of the fowls, was conceived and executed by a keen and detached observer of the foibles, not of worm-fowls, water-fowls and seed-fowls, but of his kind — even to such interchanges of amenities as he had often heard along the Thames. And for the second time Chaucer's approach to human life has been through the medium of birds, as at the zenith of his powers he comes back to them again. For in that matchless trio of which the other members are Criseyde and the Wife of Bath, it is Madame Pertelote who makes the third.

The last, if not the greatest, of the visions poems, the Prologue to the Legend of Good Women, I must regretfully pass over, together with the Knight's Tale, which, like the Troilus and Criseyde, preceded it. It is Chaucer's dealings in the Troilus with the *Filostrato* to which I wish to come, for in the Troilus, never again to lose its ascendancy, life came, like a mighty river flowing in.

From Machaut and his French contemporaries Chaucer had taken over a form which for him was relatively empty of content. In Boccaccio and Dante he found for the first time among his moderns architectonic powers which in the case of Dante were supreme, and which Boccaccio in narrative exercised with a master's skill. Moreover, in Boccaccio, and superlatively in Dante, the greatness of the form was inseparable from the richness of the content, and that content was now no longer interminable lucubrations in a vacuum, but men and women, and their actions and their fates. And in the *Filostrato* he found a story richer in possibilities than any on which he had yet exercised his powers. Into none had so many strands been woven by earlier hands, from its far-off inception in the *Iliad*, down through a provocative catalogue of names in Dares, to three of which Benoit, through one of those inscrutable promptings of genius which set in motion incalculable trains of consequence, had attached a story of faithless love. And then Boccaccio, through his own *Filocolo*, poured into it the passion of his long eventful intrigue with Maria d'Aquino. And as the inevitable consequence, his Criseida and Troilo and Pandaro *live*, as his Palamon and Arcita and Emilia never do. In the *Filostrato* Chaucer at last had flesh and blood to deal with.

What the *Filostrato* did, accordingly, was to awaken as nothing else yet had done, his own creative powers. For the Troilus is a magnificently independent reworking of Boccaccio's narrative, bearing to its original, indeed, a relation not unlike that in which *King Lear*, for example, stands to the earlier play. For Chaucer had thought deeply through Boccaccio's story before he set pen to parchment for his own. Boccaccio's Criseida is a fair and fickle woman, conventional alike in her beauty and her faithlessness; Chaucer's Criseyde, in her baffling and complex femininity remains unrivalled, save in Shakespeare and one or two of the great novelists. And by a change as simple as it is consummate in its art, Chaucer opened the way for another transformation — the metamorphosis of a conventional young man-about-town into a masterpiece of characterization which he equalled only, if I may hazard my own opinion, in the Wife of Bath. For Boccaccio's Pandaro was Criseida's cousin; Chaucer's Pandarus is her uncle. And through that simple-seeming shift, not only is the irony of the situation deepened and the tragedy enhanced, but Pandarus also becomes what a younger man could never have been — the vehicle of Chaucer's own humour and urbanity and worldly wisdom, and of his inimitable raciness of speech. Somewhere, among his courtly friends in England or in Italy or both, he had come, one feels, to know the type to which he gave immortal individuality. It is in the Troilus, too, that one also feels, again for the first time, that detachment which is also the distinctive note of the greater Canterbury Tales — that wise and urbane detachment with which Chaucer came in the end to view the human comedy. And often when Pandare speaks, one is curiously aware of something in the background — like Meredith's Comic Spirit with its 'slim feasting smile' — which is playing the game with Pandare no less urbanely and ironically than he with Troilus and Criseyde.

And those are but hints of what Chaucer's reading of life lent to his reading of Boccaccio.

Moreover, no sooner had he set out to write than his mind began to race beyond the text he was translating. In scores of stanzas, even in the first book, he will follow Boccaccio for three or four or five lines of his stanza, then go his own gate for the rest of it, as if his thought in its eagerness over-leaped Boccaccio's. And often, before he returns to his text, he has carried on alone for three, four, or a score of stanzas. And when, in the great second and third books, he comes to the heart of the drama as he conceives it, he leaves Boccaccio almost wholly aside, and the great bulk of those two crucial books is Chaucer's own. And nowhere else, save in the plan of the Canterbury Tales, does he exercise such sovereign constructive powers. Life and his reading of the great Italians had made him master of his art.

And that mastery of an art which has for its end the portrayal of life is peculiarly manifest in his dialogue. Let me read, if you will, a few of the stanzas which describe Pandare's visit to Criseyde's house:

> Whan he was come un-to his neces place,
> 'Wher is my lady?' to her folk seyde he;
> And they him tolde; and he forth in gan pace,
> And fond, two othere ladyes sete and she
> With-inne a paved parlour; and they three
> Herden a mayden reden hem the geste
> Of the Sege of Thebes, whyl hem leste.

Quod Pandarus, 'ma dame, God you see,
With al your book and al the companye!'
'Ey, uncle myn, welcome y-wis,' quod she,
And up she roos, and by the hond in hye
She took him faste, and seyde, 'this night thrye,
To goode mote it turne, of yow I mette!'
And with that word she doun on bench him sette.

'Ye, nece, ye shal fare wel the bet,
If god wole, al this yeer,' quod Pandarus;
'But I am sory that I have yow let
To herknen of your book ye preysen thus;
For goddes love, what seith it? tel it us.
Is it of love? O, some good ye me lere!'
'Uncle,' quod she, 'Your maistresse is not here!'

With that they gonnen laughe, and tho she seyde,
'This romaunce is of Thebes, that we rede' . . .

'As ever thryve I,' quod this Pandarus,
'Yet coude I telle a thing to doon you pleye.'
'Now uncle dere,' quod she, 'tel it us
For goddes love; is than th' assege aweye?
I am of Grekes so ferd that I deye.'
'Nay, nay,' quod he, 'as ever mote I thryve!
It is a thing wel bet than swiche fyve.'

'Ye, holy god!' quod she, 'what thing is that?
What? bet than swiche fyve? ey, nay, y-wis!
For al this world ne can I reden what
It sholde been; som jape, I trowe, is this;
And but your-selven telle us what it is
My wit is for to arede it al to lene;
As help me god, I noot nat what ye mene.'

'And I your borow, ne never shal, for me,
This thing be told to yow, as mote I thryve!'
'And why so, uncle myn? why so?' quod she.
'By god,' quod he, 'that wole I telle as blyve;
For prouder womman were ther noon on-lyve,
And ye it wiste, in al the toun of Troye;
I jape nought, as ever have I joye!'

It would be hard to find even in the Canterbury
Tales a more superb handling of dialogue than that,
with its swift touch and go of actual talk, its subtle
nuances, and its seeming impromptu which only a
master's technique could achieve.

And in nothing that he ever wrote did his possession at once of the scholar's and the artist's gifts
stand him in better stead than in his weaving into
one the complex strands which underlay his story.
And as he wrote, phrases and ideas, Boccaccio's or
his own, kept calling up to his memory associated
fragments of his reading, and the *Divine Comedy*,
and the *Convito*, and the *Teseide*, and a sonnet of
Petrarch, and Ovid, Virgil, Statius and Boethius,
and the *Roman de la Rose* and the *Roman d'Eneas* and
even Machaut himself (to name no more) contribute
to the sense which we have in the Troilus of a richness like God's plenty, which pervades the poem.

When Chaucer ended the Troilus, he was in
possession of a mastered art. To the question which
I asked in the beginning — What aside from genius
made the poet of the greater Canterbury Tales? —
I have attempted, within my limits of time and
understanding, to give an answer. The supreme art

of that crowning achievement had been learned through the independent exercise of his own powers upon given materials — upon form and content of conventional types or specific poems, which the accident of courtly connexions or business in Italy had offered. And through the poet's gift of seeing the latent possibilities in everything he touched, and through the scholar's passion for facts, and through his own invincible eagerness of spirit which spared no pains, his masters and his models slipped steadily into the background, and on the threshold of the Canterbury Tales the theme towards which his face was turned was *life* — that life above all which through years of intimate contact with it he had learned to know; not French life nor Italian life, but English. And instead of any longer filling empty forms or reconstructing full ones, he drew straight from life a framework of his own — the one form in all the world to give free play to his disciplined and ripened powers, and room for all that wealth of reading and experience with which this tale began. And as if with one lingering look behind, he begins his masterpiece — I wish I knew whether he so meant it — with an exquisite *ave atque vale*:

> Whan that Aprille with his shoures sote
> The droghte of Marche hath perced to the rote,
> And bathed every veyne in swich licour,
> Of which vertu engendred is the flour;
> Whan Zephirus eek with his swete breeth
> Inspired hath in every holt and heeth
> The tendre croppes ...

and on through the lovely lines still redolent of their April freshness after five hundred years. That is the stock introduction — *sed quantum mutatus ab illo* — to a hundred love-vision poems! But instead of ushering in Plaisance and Esperance and Douce Pensée and their crew of fellow abstractions, it opens the door of the Tabard Inn to Harry Bailly and the Wife of Bath and the Miller and the Pardoner and their goodly fellowship. There could be no better symbol than those opening lines of the continuity, through steadily maturing powers, of Chaucer's art. And it is that continuity of evolution, up to the full flowering of his genius in the Canterbury Tales, that I have essayed to describe.

Two Readings of Earth

Two Readings of Earth

THE terms of this Lectureship [1] impose upon every lecturer who holds it a significant restriction. Only the *recent*, in literature or science, may, under the deed of gift, afford the theme. But the recent, as such, has a singular attribute. It moves, an eternal fugitive, along an endless track, for ever becoming and, as it becomes, for ever ceasing to be. Every moment, from the Dinosaurs to Darwin, has been recent in its turn, and every vivid one of them is so no more. And behind us, as the wingèd chariot that bears us hurries on, poetry, prose, drama, and the miracles of science which are today the latest things, stream back to join that ineluctably receding multitude. For our recent — 'nor all our piety nor wit Shall lure it back' — will be the antiquated, ancient, even obsolete to other speakers (soon enough!) upon the no less transitory recent of their day. That is the most exquisite of Time's little ironies — this synchronous recession and progression of the present with all its works, as if in some fantastic fashion we were simultaneously backward

[1] The Francis Bergen Lectures, Yale University.

streaming wake and flying sail. The limitation laid upon these lectures is in effect a peremptory *carpe diem*.

> Gather ye rosebuds while ye may,
> Old Time is still a-flying:
> And this same flower that smiles today,
> Tomorrow will be dying.

Perhaps! But at least the recent will never be recent again — never again can be seen as we alone can see it. And therein lies, I take it, the significance of this Foundation.

I have chosen, then, two Englishmen — one dead since 1909, the other living and still writing at the age of eighty-five [1] — whose pre-eminence among contemporary men of letters will be questioned, I suppose, by few. Both are novelists, both poets; and in both verse has supplemented prose in the expression of a deeply felt philosophy of life for which the more accustomed medium proved inadequate. Both read with peculiarly sensitive vision the face of earth and sky; both read with still more penetrating eye the hidden sense behind the shows; and both have given voice to their readings with superb indifference to conventional acceptances. They have in common a profound sincerity and the gift of looking facts indomitably in the face; in the interpretation of their facts they differ, yet not without significant concurrences. They are both supremely of their time, which still is ours; and I for one believe that both have in them elements of

[1] This was written in 1924.

immortality. I have no intention of subjecting them to rigorous critical analysis. They have seen with a poet's eye, whether writing in prose or in verse, the beauty of earth, and they have striven to discern its meaning. And their readings of earth, as concretely as it is in my power to give them, will constitute the burden of my theme.

I

In the first edition of *Wessex Poems* are incorporated some thirty 'rough sketches,' as Hardy calls them, each signed with the monogram ⅏. Solitary figures black against a sea of light, or outlined against endless space, or walking lonely roads that stretch into infinity; a field of English graves beside a mound that was a Roman amphitheatre, across the pagan edge of which peer tips of Christian spires; a brave little caterpillar line of soldiers; 'the wayless wet gray ground of Waterloo' — an empty, shadow-haunted plain in spectral light; a beautiful dead form beneath a winding-sheet; a flaming comet; a broken key — latent in those dozen emblems are the themes which walked like ghosts the corridors of Hardy's brain. But there is one of them which epitomizes him as that poignant little sketch of Blake's — the tiny figure starting up its gossamer stair to grasp the moon, with the legend under it: I WANT, I WANT — is eloquent of Blake. It is the frontispiece to a sequence of four poems entitled *She, to Him*. A vast, dim moorland rises against the rim of the world, its skyline cutting the misty radiance of a setting sun, whose streamers are like the spokes of some gigantic cosmic wheel. Up the huge shoulder of the heath winds the white, serpentine line of a road, and down the road, discernible only against its pallor, are moving side by side two shadowy human shapes. The moor is elemental as the frosts and rains that carved it; the road is old as the prehistoric dead whose feet first wore its winding track. And He and She, as Hardy lends us eyes to see them, are woven in one web with dying suns and earth's diurnal sway and ghostly presences.

Now beside that set Egdon Heath, with its 'aged highway,' and 'its sombre stretch of rounds and hollows that seem to rise and meet the evening gloom,' and the solitary human figure on its summit, motionless as the immobile earth beneath its feet. That figure, like the two on the slope of the moorland in the sketch, turns at last to go, and Hardy characterizes its descent in ten pregnant words: 'it descended... *with the glide of a waterdrop down a bud*,' as if the breathing mortal were co-elemental with insensate things, and one, in its impotence, with their fatality. Read in its context of enormous, brooding presences, that lovely, fate-laden phrase becomes the very epitome of Hardy's irony. For the essence of that irony lies in a pervading sense of the infinitesimal littleness of the human atom on the face of its vast, inanimate, yet somehow sentient, watching, immanent environment. Hardy's earth, in a word, is a *haunted* place, and if I can make that clear we shall reach in the end, I think, the distinctive element in a daring and powerfully individual conception of the universe.

And first of all, the world as Hardy sees it is, to a degree perhaps unparalleled, a world of the two twilights and of night — a world in which 'light thickens,' and 'good things of day begin to droop and drowse.' 'The place became full of a watchful intentness now; for when other things sank brooding to sleep the heath appeared slowly to awake and listen' — and everyone knows the Lucretian grandeur with which that theme unfolds throughout the tragedy. But there is the sister twilight, dawn, and that is sentient too. 'The whole enormous landscape bore that impress of reserve, taciturnity, and hesitation which is usual just before day. . . . Presently the night wind died out, and the quivering little pools in the cup-like hollows of the stones lay still' — and in another intent, considering twilight another tragedy draws to its close. We move with Hardy at life's crucial moments through a taciturn, brooding, crepuscular world, in which dread things awaited come to pass, as if the waiting and the coming were, through some unconscious power that works through each, one thing. For dawn and twilight are more than the daily roll of earth from light to darkness and from darkness into light. They are inscrutable potencies and dim sentiences. 'In the twilight of the morning light seems active, darkness passive; in the twilight of evening it is the darkness which is active and crescent, and the light which is the drowsy reverse.' That pregnant sentence ushers in the walks through ghostly dawns which wrought their will on Angel Clare and Tess. And page after page is pervaded with the sense of infinite weavings going on as day dies or is born. Michelangelo's Dawn and Twilight, dreaming with strange secrets in their drowsy eyes, are kith and kin to Hardy's disembodied, potent effluences of an earth that hovers between sleep and wake.

But between twilight and dawn night lies over the earth, and night to Hardy is alive with vast, grotesque projections of pigmy human doings against the endless reaches of the world. The upper air is a screen upon which trivial objects throw dilated 'phantoms of sublimity.' Two, He and She, walk out with a perforated lantern, and 'the patterns of the air-holes in the top of the lantern rise to the mist overhead, where they appear of giant size, as if reaching the tent-shaped sky.' Another two, at another fated moment, have met by lantern-light, and the lantern standing on the ground betwixt them, and throwing its gleam among the blades of long damp grass 'with the effect of a large glow-worm ... radiated upwards into their faces, and sent over half the plantation gigantic shadows of both man and woman' — shadows that fled, 'distorted and mangled upon the tree-trunks, till they wasted to nothing.' It is not accidental that these mocking shapes with their fantastic discrepancy between the object and the shadow walk side by side with mortals through the night. The grotesqueries of light and shadow are among the most effective instruments of Hardy's irony. The bonfires on Egdon Heath — the heath down which Eustacia had just glided like a waterdrop — work metamorphoses upon both sky and earth. 'Tufts of fire . . . glowing scarlet-red from the shade, like wounds in a black hide; Maenades, with winy faces and blown hair,' they 'tinctured the silent bosom of the clouds above them and lit up their ephemeral caves, which seemed thenceforth to become scalding caldrons.' But on the faces of the circumambient earthlings they played more impish tricks. 'All was unstable; quivering as leaves, evanescent as lightning. Shadowy eye-sockets, deep as those of a death's head, suddenly turned into pits of lustre; a lantern-jaw was cavernous, then it was shining; wrinkles were emphasized to ravines . . . nostrils were dark wells . . . eyeballs glowed like little lanterns.' Night, for Hardy, peoples earth, through its reflections and refractions, with spectral parodies of breathing flesh and blood, as it is night which, in its huge, impassive Immanence, engulfs their pitiful hopes and fears. 'The night came in, and took up its place there, unconcerned and indifferent; the night which had already swallowed up his happiness, and was now digesting it listlessly; and was ready to swallow up the happiness of a thousand other people with as little disturbance or change of mien.' Among all the nights of all the poets there is none to match that terrible, remorseless, tranquil Thing.

Moreover, it is night which stirs in us the consciousness of imperturbable, resistless cosmic energies which hold us, helpless as a drop of water, in their unresting sway. Sometimes at midnight 'the roll of the world eastward is almost a palpable movement,' and you can 'long and quietly watch your stately progress through the stars.' 'Above the dark margin of the earth,' as Bathsheba Everdene sat by the wayside, 'appeared foreshores and promontories of coppery cloud . . . and the unresting world wheeled her round to a contrasting prospect eastward, in the shape of indecisive and palpitating stars.' And down in the Nether Glooms the dead

> . . . hear the axle grind
> Round and round
> Of the great world.

Moreover, in this planetary consciousness of ours the earth itself towers looming over us, or stretches off to the steep brink of space. 'The distant rims of the world' are our horizon; the forms about the bonfires on the summit of the heath stand as if 'in some radiant upper storey of the world'; and in the tremendous Third Part of *The Dynasts* the Spirit of the Years who knows the Immanent Will residing at 'the Back of Things' asks the Spirit of the Pities:

> Must I again reveal It as It hauls
> The halyards of the world?

Only Lucretius can vie with Hardy in the sombre grandeur of his universe, and the *flammantia moenia mundi* might almost have come from Hardy's pen.

And this sense of the immensities of time and space is wrought into the very fibre of his pondering imagination. The stupendous history of the stellar universe, from scattered haze to nebulous centre and solid mass, is re-enacted in the evolutions of a swarm of bees; the ruddy glow from a kiln mouth shines over the floor 'with the streaming horizontality of the setting sun'; the 'glistening ripple of gossamer webs' is 'like the track of moonlight on the sea.' The yearly coming of the frost is thrown against the background of the elemental forces which sweep across the trackless spaces about the turning axle of the world: 'after this season . . . came a spell of dry frost, when strange birds from behind the North Pole began to arrive silently on the upland of Flintcomb-Ash; gaunt spectral creatures with tragical eyes — eyes which had witnessed scenes of cataclysmal horror in inaccessible polar regions of a magnitude such as no human being had ever conceived, in curdling temperatures that no man could endure; which had beheld the crash of icebergs and the slide of snow-hills by the shooting light of the Aurora; been half blinded by the whirl of colossal storms and terraqueous distortions; and retained the expression of feature that such scenes had engendered.' And with dumb impassivity, like twilight or the night, these nameless visitants watch the trivial movements of two turnip-diggers in the fields below them, who with like impassivity disturbed the clods.

But more than night and twilight with their brood of phantoms walk the world as sentient things. The Past walks with them as a presence that eternally persists, impalpable, yet, like the aged heath, somehow intent and watchful. It is not I who am fabricating Hardy's haunted world. It builds itself up before us as through a thousand hints we catch glimpses of the strange, profound, and baffling universe of his perception or conception — which, who can say? And in that universe in a sense that one deeply feels, whatever the cold intellect may think, nothing ever truly dies. The upper air — and this was never more intelligible than now, when over seas and continents the encircling atmosphere is a pulsing thoroughfare of disembodied voices — the upper air holds everlastingly all that through endless time has been committed to it.

> Here's the mould of a musical bird long passed from light,
> Which over the earth before man came was winging;
> There's a contralto voice I heard last night,
> That lodges in me still with its sweet singing.

> Such a dream is Time that the coo of this ancient bird
> Has perished not, but is blent, or will be blending
> Mid visionless wilds of space with the voice that I heard,
> In the full-fugued song of the universe unending.

But it is earth in which we earthlings are undying, the perpetual participants in the blind processes we call life.

> Portion of this yew
> Is a man my grandsire knew,

Bosomed here at its foot:
This branch may be his wife,
A ruddy human life
Now turned to a green shoot.

These grasses must be made
Of her who often prayed,
Last century, for repose;
And the fair girl long ago
Whom I often tried to know
May be entering this rose.

So, they are not underground,
But as nerves and veins abound
In the growths of upper air,
And they feel the sun and rain,
And the energy again
That made them what they were!

And there are survivals yet more secret and in-
tangible:

I am the family face;
Flesh perishes, I live on,
Projecting trait and trace
Through time to times anon,
And leaping from place to place
Over oblivion.

The years-heired feature that can
In curve and voice and eye
Despise the human span
Of durance — that is I;
The eternal thing in man,
That heeds no call to die.

And so, on the age-old soil of Wessex, as a ghostly
co-weaver in the web of human destiny, there lives

through its ancient vestiges the immemorial pagan Past. The plateaux are 'bosomed with semi-globular tumuli — as if Cybele the Many-breasted were supinely extended there.' The Roman Road runs straight and bare across the heath, 'near where, men say, once stood the Fane to Venus, on the Down' — the road 'where Legions had wayfared.' The mocking bonfires on the heath are lineal descendants of the British pyres whose ashes still lie fresh and undisturbed beneath the barrows. Eustacia Vye, who glided down the barrow, is as pagan and nocturnal as the heath itself. And when the Roman shrine at Aquae Sulis was uncovered,

> ... a warm air came up from underground,
> And a flutter, as of a filmy shape unsepulchred,
> That collected itself, and waited, and looked around:
> Nothing was seen, but utterances could be heard:
> Those of the goddess whose shrine was beneath the pile
> Of the God with the baldachined altar overhead.

Then, when the faint, fluttery pagan chidings ceased,

> And the olden dark hid the cavities late laid bare,
> ... all was suspended and soundless as before,
> Except for a gossamery noise fading off in the air.

Grim humour, if you will, this last; but it, like the rest, is a symbol of something which to Hardy (and to most of us who think) is a profound reality: the δύναμις ζωῆς ἀκαταλύτου — the power of an indissoluble life — possessed and exercised by the undying Past.

But earth is to Hardy a haunted spot in a far more intimate, personal way. I know no poetry so pervaded as his with a sense of the continued presence of the dead, nor is there another body of verse in the world, I think, in which that sense is conveyed to us with such intolerable poignancy and beauty. It is a strange paradox. No poet of our day is, in his sharp breach with tradition, so intensely of his time as Thomas Hardy; and no poet writing today would have been so utterly at home on earth a thousand years ago. No one but Hardy could have written the passing strange and moving lines in which the souls of the men of Wessex slain in the Boer war come home to the ancient promontory on which ghosts have walked since the Stone Age — come with

> A whirr, as of wings
> Waved by mighty-vanned flies,
> Or by night-moths of measureless size,
> And in softness and smoothness well-nigh beyond hearing
> Of corporal things.

No one but Hardy could have written this about 'Old Furniture':

> I see the hands of the generations
> That owned each shiny familiar thing
> In play on its knobs and indentations,
> And with its ancient fashioning
> Still dallying:
>
> Hands behind hands, growing paler and paler,
> As in a mirror a candle flame

Shows images of itself, each frailer
As it recedes. . . .

And all about us there are ghostly whispers:

'Gone,' I call them, gone for good, that group of local hearts
and heads;
Yet at mothy curfew-tide,
And at midnight when the noon-heat breathes it back from
walls and leads,
They've a way of whispering to me — fellow-wight who yet
abide —
In the muted, measured note
Of a ripple under archways, or a lone cave's stillicide.

But far more often love and death walk hand in
hand along frequented ways:

My spirit will not haunt the mound
Above my breast,
But travel, memory-possessed,
To where my tremulous being found
Life largest, best.

My phantom-footed shape will go
When nightfall grays
Hither and thither along the ways
I and another used to know
In backward days.

And there you'll find me, if a jot
You still should care
For me, and for my curious air;
If otherwise, then I shall not,
For you, be there.

And the dead are 'there' in memory, and in a
hundred poems which probe to the quick, there

unfolds, touched with grave pity and phrased with stern restraint, the human tragedy of belated re-collection.

> 'Why do you stand in the dripping rye,
> Cold-lipped, unconscious, wet to the knee,
> When there are firesides near?' said I.
> 'I told him I wished him dead,' said she.

> 'Yea, cried it in my haste to one
> Whom I had loved, whom I well loved still;
> And die he did.   And I hate the sun,
> And stand here lonely, aching, chill;

> 'Stand waiting, waiting under skies
> That blow reproach, the while I see
> The rocks sheer off to where he lies
> Wrapt in a peace withheld from me!'

Or this:

> How she would have loved
> A party today! —
> Bright-hatted and gloved,
> With table and tray
> And chairs on the lawn
> Her smiles would have shone
> With welcomings. . . . But
> She is shut, she is shut
>   From friendship's spell
>   In the jailing shell
>   Of her tiny cell.

> And she would have sought
> With a child's eager glance
> The shy snowdrops brought
> By the new year's advance,
> And peered in the rime

Of Candlemas-time
For crocuses . . . chanced
It that she were not tranced
    From sights she loved best;
    Wholly possessed
    By an infinite rest!

In their penetrating vision into the sealed yet
tenanted chambers of the heart no less than for
their noble austerity of rhythm and diction, the
later poems are among the things which men will
not let die. And in them the Ironic Spirits, audible
still, are yielding to the Spirit of the Pities.

And now we come to the central mystery, in
which all these scattered intimations of shadowy
presences cohere — to the Infinite Haunter of a
universe that is Its troubled dream.

For all the ghostly shapes that stalk the twilight
and the night — projections of human finitude
against the unseeing sky, or of the changeless Past
upon the fleeting Present — are but the faintest
adumbrations of that stupendous panorama which
unrolls through *The Dynasts,* inexorable and un-
hurried as the nightly revolution of the stars. There
is in literature no conception like it. The colossal
stage is now the Earth and now the Overworld;
the action is the vast convulsion of the Napoleonic
wars; the actors are the innumerable throng of
human participants in the cataclysm, and Phantom
Intelligences of the Overworld. And these Intelligences are the Shade of the Earth, and the Ancient
Spirit of the Years, and the Spirit of the Pities,

and Spirits Sinister and Ironic — mocking Mephistophelian Voices, and 'the passionless Insight of the Ages,' and 'the Universal Sympathy of human nature'; and they view (and we with them) the human scene from the towering upper storeys of the world, or else take human form, and, like the ancient Adversary, walk, mocking or in pity, to and fro upon the earth. I suspect that there has never been in English letters, at least since Shakespeare, a genius more essentially pictorial than Thomas Hardy's, and in *The Dynasts* it is at the culmination of its power. All the pomp and circumstance of courts and chancellories, all the glory and (depicted with unsparing realism) all the gruesome spectacles of war, all the little human lives in hamlets and on highways drawn without their will into the vortex — all these pass before us in vivid, incredible profusion, as if thrown by some magical cinematograph upon an endlessly unfolding screen. Nor are we ever left long at close quarters, where the shows of earth loom large. There comes at intervals a recession of the point of vision into endless space, and this is the instrument of Hardy's most relentless irony. For suddenly, as the shifting spectacle unrolls, we are rapt to vast aërial distances, to look down on earth from 'architraves of sunbeam-smitten cloud' with the eyes of passionless or pitying or sardonic Phantoms, whose vision is cosmic, not terrestrial. And not even Swift himself has more remorselessly depicted human littleness.

The Fore Scene in the Overworld sets the panorama moving:

> The nether sky opens, and Europe is disclosed as a prone and emaciated figure, the Alps shaping like a backbone, and the branching mountain-chains like ribs, the peninsular plateau of Spain forming a head. Broad and lengthy lowlands stretch from the north of France across Russia like a grey-green garment hemmed by the Ural mountains and the glistening Arctic Ocean.
>
> The point of view then sinks downwards through space, and draws near to the surface of the perturbed countries, where the peoples ... are seen writhing, crawling, heaving, and vibrating in their various cities and nationalities. ...
>
> A new and penetrating light descends on the spectacle, enduing men and things with a seeming transparency, and exhibiting as one organism the anatomy of life and movement in all humanity and vitalized matter included in the display.

The Spirit of the Years interprets the amazing spectacle; 'the anatomy of the Immanent Will disappears'; and the action begins.

Then in measured succession glimpse follows terrible glimpse.

> A bird's-eye perspective is revealed of the peninsular tract of Portuguese territory lying between the shining pool of the Tagus on the east, and the white-frilled Atlantic lifting rhythmically on the west. ... Innumerable human figures are busying themselves like cheese-mites ... digging ditches, piling stones, felling trees. ... Three reddish-grey streams of marching men loom out to the north. ... These form the English

army.... Looked down upon, their motion seems peristaltic and vermicular, like that of three caterpillars.... The Dumb Show ends, and the point of view sinks to the earth.

The huge procession along the great road across Europe from Vienna to Munich and from Munich westerly to France dwindles to 'a puny concatenation of specks,' like 'a file of ants crawling along a strip of garden-matting'; the battle of Leipzig, as the Leipzig clocks imperturbably strike nine, is seen only as 'amorphous drifts, clouds, and waves of conscious atoms, surging and rolling together'; before the battle of Wagram 'a species of simmer ... pervades the living spectacle.' Before the battle of Waterloo, 'as the curtain of the mist is falling, the point of vision soars again.... From all parts of Europe long and sinister black files are crawling hitherward in serpentine lines, like slowworms through grass. They are the advancing armies of the Allies.' That is the impending cataclysm seen *sub specie aeternitatis* by the Phantoms of the Overworld. But the lines march over an Underworld — a world likewise of worms to their mortal sight, as they are worms to the sight above:

> The mole's tunnelled chambers are crushed by wheels,
> The lark's eggs scattered, their owners fled;
> And the hedgehog's household the sapper unseals.
>
> The snail draws in at the terrible tread,
> But in vain; he is crushed by the felloe-rim;
> The worm asks what can be overhead,

And wriggles deep from a scene so grim,
And guesses him safe; for he does not know
What a foul red flood will be soaking him!

Waterloo between the passionless Intelligences and
the Worms — that is Lilliput and Brobdingnag
rolled into one with quintessential mockery.

But the most pitiless irony of all is in another
vision. Again we are 'high amongst the clouds,
which, opening and shutting fitfully to the wind,
reveal the earth as a confused expanse merely.'
On the far land-verge is seen 'An object like a
dun-piled caterpillar, Shuffling its length in painful
heaves along.' It is 'the Army Which once was
called the Grand; now in retreat From Moscow's
muteness' — burning Moscow, seen from the clouds
in the blackness to the north as 'a lurid, malig-
nant star.' And the Recording Angels who are
chronicling, stage by stage, the flight, set down
their closing entry:

And so and thus it nears Smolensko's walls,
And, stayed its hunger, starts anew its crawls,
.Till floats down one white morsel, which appals.

And that white morsel, the veriest pigmy among all
the objects in the whole colossal panorama, is the
most terrible. For (the laconic comment goes on),
'What has floated down from the sky upon the
Army is a flake of snow. Then come another and
another, till natural features ... are confounded,
and all is phantasmal grey and white. The caterpillar shape still creeps laboriously nearer, but

instead of increasing in size by the rules of perspective, it gets more attenuated, and there are left upon the ground behind it minute parts of itself, which are speedily flaked over, and remain as white pimples by the wayside.' Beyond that last merciless figure, irony cannot go.

I have given but the barest inkling of the conception which underlies Hardy's amazing epic drama. But I know nothing in its fashion more Titanic than that huge stage on which no longer the stars in secret influence comment, but Phantasms — Phantasms which are themselves hovering projections, like the dilated pattern of lantern-rays against the tent-shaped sky, of the finite Intelligences resident in the cheese-mite animalcules below. It is irony within irony, for the watchers and the watched are each the simulacrum of the other, and alike inhere in — what?

And now we reach the heart of Hardy's *Weltanschauung*, the Haunter of Haunters in his ghost-frequented universe. For in and through, above and below the human spectacle weave 'the ubiquitous urgings of the Immanent Will.' And that spectacle is but 'one flimsy riband of Its web,'

> Whose furthest hem and selvage may extend
> To where the roars and plashings of the flames
> Of earth-invisible suns swell noisily,
> And onward into ghastly gulfs of sky,
> Where hideous presences churn through the dark —
> Monsters of magnitude without a shape,
> Hanging amid deep wells of nothingness.

And the 'dreaming, dark, dumb Thing' that weaves unwittingly the tiny, tragi-comic human web is immanent no less in that stupendous flux. But — and this is the element of profound significance — that 'viewless, voiceless Turner of the Wheel' is a Somnambulist who may one day awake; it is the blind dimly groping after vision, the unconscious struggling painfully up to consciousness, as we who are of a piece with it agonize back to our sense of self from the black abyss of a swoon. And earth and the unsounded depths of space beyond the flaming barriers of the world must be read as a fleeting moment in the unfolding of that unfathomable cosmic drama. 'Ungefähr sagt das der Pfarrer auch, Nur mit ein Bischen andern Worten' — for another, who at moments was among the world's great poets, saw it too: 'For we know that the whole creation groaneth and travaileth in pain together until now, waiting for the revealing of the sons of God.' And what the sons of God are, who can say? But as for the *waiting*, Paul and Thomas Hardy are at one:

> At last I entered a long dark gallery,
>   Catacomb-lined; and ranged at the side
>   Were the bodies of men from far and wide
> Who, motion past, were nevertheless not dead.

> 'The sense of waiting here strikes strong;
> Everyone's waiting, waiting, it seems to me;
>   What are you waiting for so long? —
>   What is to happen?' I said.

'O we are waiting for one called God,' said they,
  '(Though by some the Will, or Force, or Laws;
  And, vaguely, by some, the Ultimate Cause;)
Waiting for him to see us before we are clay.
  Yes; waiting, waiting, for God *to know it*.' ...
  'To know what?' questioned I.
'To know how things have been going on earth and below it:
  It is clear he must know some day.'
  I thereon asked them why.

'Since he made us humble pioneers
Of himself in consciousness of Life's tears,
It needs no mighty prophecy
To tell that what he could mindlessly show
  His creatures, he himself will know.

'By some still close-cowled mystery
We have reached feeling faster than he,
But he will overtake us anon,
  If the world goes on.'

Nor is that dramatic 'Fragment' all. 'Hap,' 'Nature's Questioning,' 'Doom and She,' 'By the Earth's Corpse,' 'The Sleep-Worker,' 'New Year's Eve,' 'God's Education,' 'God's Funeral,' 'The Blow' — through that stern unflinching succession of poems, and through the long, inexorable evolution of *The Dynasts*, and through those strange broodings of intent and watchful twilights, ebbs and flows that sense of a waiting universe.

'I have finished another year,' said God,
  'In grey, green, white, and brown;
I have strewn the leaf upon the sod,
Sealed up the worm within the clod,
  And let the last sun down.'

TWO READINGS OF EARTH

'And what's the good of it?' I said —

and after question and answer,

> He sank to raptness as of yore,
>   And opening New Year's Day
> Wove it by rote as theretofore,
> And went on working evermore
>   In his unweeting way.

But over against that must be set this:

> And if it prove that no man did,
> And that the Inscrutable, the Hid,
>   Was cause alone
> Of this foul crash our lives amid,
>
> I'll go in due time, and forget
> In some deep graveyard's oubliette
>   The thing whereof I groan,
> And cease from troubling; thankful yet
>
> Time's finger should have stretched to show
> No aimful author's was the blow
>   That swept as prone,
> But the Immanent Doer's That doth not know,
>
> Which in some age unguessed of us
> May lift Its blinding incubus,
>   And see, and own:
> 'It grieves me I did thus and thus!'

Nor is it accident that these next lines fall from the lips of the Spirit of the Pities:

> Yet It may wake and understand
> Ere Earth unshape, know all things, and
> With knowledge use a painless hand,
>   A painless hand!

On that note the matchless After Scene of *The Dynasts* ends:

> O Immanence, That reasonest not
> In putting forth all things begot,
> Thou build'st Thy house in space — for what?
> O Loveless, Hateless! — past the sense
> Of kindly eyed benevolence,
> To what tune danceth this Immense? ...

> Heaving dumbly
> As we deem,
> Moulding numbly
> As in dream,
> Apprehending not how fare the sentient subjects of Its scheme.

> Nay; — shall not Its blindness break?
> Yea, must not Its heart awake,
> Promptly tending
> To Its mending
> In a genial germing purpose, and for loving-kindness' sake?

> Should It never
> Curb or cure
> Aught whatever
> Those endure
> Whom It quickens, let them darkle to extinction swift and sure.

> But — a stirring thrills the air
> Like to sounds of joyance there
> That the rages
> Of the ages
> Shall be cancelled, and deliverance offered from the darts that were,
> Consciousness the Will informing, till It fashion all things fair!

And there may fitly end this fragmentary abstract of a very great poet's reading of earth. What you and I may think of its validity is for the moment quite beside the point. It stands, in its stark grandeur and its sad sincerity, among the imperishable things.

II

And now we enter another world, *a riveder le stelle* — a world of windswept daylight and the lucid upper spaces of the air. For Meredith's reading of earth stands over against Hardy's in vivid contrast, and that antithesis, at whatever cost of omitted loveliness, must rigidly define our choice and limit our consideration.

And first of all, Hardy's glory of darkness yields place to an earth above which, a luminous effluence, brightness lingers. For no poet whom I can think of is so dear a lover of light as Meredith — not light that throbs, like Shelley's, ethereal and unlocalized in the intense inane, but light that lies like a bright robe upon earth. Even darkness itself is light about us, with 'that fire in the night which lights the night and draws the night to look at it'; and the radiance in which Meredith's daylight world is bathed is too pervasive to admit of illustration here. But his unhaunted twilights that come and go in beauty confront, like spirits of light for love of earth come down to dwell among us, the spectral presences that wait and watch in Hardy's world. Even the human face, in that intimate interpenetration of earth and man which is the essence of Meredith's unique imaginative vision, is invested with the loveliness of dawn and evening. 'Her face was like the quiet morning of a winter day.' 'Her face was like an Egyptian sky fronting night.' And that same sense of intimacy between earth and man pervades the sunsets and the dawns which lend to earth 'grave heavenliness,' and humanize the alien sky. The twilights of the two interpreters are visitants from two divergent worlds of thought and feeling, and in the words which Meredith uses of the fountain and the rill, 'I know not which has most to tell.'

Moreover, through both Hardy's and Meredith's twilights moves the moon. Hardy's moon is apt to be a goblin in the sky:

And green-rheumed clouds were hurrying past where mute
    and cold it globed
  Like a drifting dolphin's eye seen through a lapping wave.

At the shiver of morning, a little before the false dawn,
  The moon was at the window-square,
  Deedily brooding in deformed decay —
  The curve hewn off her cheek as by an adze.

And the moon who peeps in at windows reads her earth with merciless finality:

'What do you think of it, Moon,
    As you go?
  Is Life much, or no?'

'O, I think of it, often think of it
    As a show
  God ought surely to shut up soon,
    As I go.'

But to Meredith it is an intimate presence among the fair, familiar things of earth. 'The moon ... had now topped the cedar, and was pure silver. ... And in the West, facing it, was an arch of twilight and tremulous rose; as if a spirit hung there over the shrouded sun'; 'A sleepy fire of early moonlight hung through the dusky fir-branches'; 'A pillar of dim silver rain fronted the moon on the hills'; 'Over the flowering hawthorn the moon stood like a wind-blown white rose of the heavens'; 'With slow foot The low rosed moon, the face of Music mute, Begins among her silent bars to climb.' In each of the two poets the moon is of a piece with the subtly fashioned universe of blending thought and imagery of which it is a part. To love both Meredith and Hardy is more than a test of catholicity. It means possession of the power to apprehend at once the poignant beauty and the nameless dread that hand in hand walk with us through the world.

Death itself is conceived by Meredith in terms of brightness falling from the air:

> I hang upon the boundaries like light
> Along the hills when downward goes the day.
> I enter the black boat
> Upon the wide grey sea,
> Where all her set suns float.

But oftener — and now we come very close to Thomas Hardy — death, like life, is but a phase of the eternal metamorphoses of earth, to be met with

TWO READINGS OF EARTH

> Fortitude quiet as Earth's
> At the shedding of leaves.

'Teach me,' Meredith exclaims,

> Teach me to feel myself the tree,
>   And not the withered leaf.
> Fixed am I and await the dark to-be.
>   And O, green bounteous Earth! ...
> Death shall I shrink from, loving thee?
> Into the breast that gives the rose,
>   Shall I with shuddering fall?

Set beside that the no less lovely, infinitely hopeless requiem of Hardy:

> May his sad sunken soul merge into nought
> Meekly and gently as a breeze at eve.

And for Meredith too the moving air is merged with the passing of our frail mortality:

> A wind sways the pines,
>   And below
> Not a breath of wild air;
> Still as the mosses that glow
> On the flooring and over the lines
> Of the roots here and there.
> The pine-tree drops its dead;
> They are quiet, as under the sea.
> Overhead, overhead
> Rushes life in a race,
> As the clouds the clouds chase;
>   And we go,
> And we drop like the fruits of the tree,
>   Even we,
>   Even so.

And in these lines we reach another of those presences which, like the light, are all-pervasive and instinct with meaning.

For as in no other writer whom I know the great winds sweep through Meredith's pages, prose and verse. There is something tenuous and ghostly about Hardy's winds. The breezes filter through twigs 'as through a strainer; it was as if the night sang dirges with clenched teeth.' The 'plaintive November wind . . . is a worn whisper, dry and papery'; it plays its 'mewling music on the strings Of . . . shipmasts,' or 'mooes and mouths the chimney like a horn'; 'the dead and dry carcasses of leaves tap the ground.' But the wind which blows through Meredith's world is the great South-wester with its glory of flying clouds — 'the charioted South-west at full charge behind his panting coursers.' Every reader of the novels and the poems knows those 'day[s] of the cloud in fleets'; days 'Of wedded white and blue, that sail Immingled, with a footing ray In shadow-sandals down [the] vale'; days when, as in the magnificent *Ode to the Spirit of Earth in Autumn*, 'the bull-voiced oak is battling' with the glorious South-west that plunges on it with the pressure of a sea. The wind that passeth and cleanseth; the south wind that quieteth the earth; the fair weather that cometh with terrible majesty out of the north; the balancings of the clouds — all those swift angels of the air on which the Hebrew poet pondered are to Meredith what the brooding intentness of night is to Hardy's sombre gaze. And they stand in close relation to a conception more deeply characteristic still.

For over and over again we are met as we read with a 'sense of wings uplifting' (to use Coleridge's splendid phrase), and even of an upward lift of earth itself: 'A sharp breath of air had passed along the dews. . . . The sky, set with very dim distant stars, was in grey light round a small brilliant moon. Every space of earth lifted clear to her; the woodland listened; and in the bright silence the nightingales sang loud.' Hardy's earth lifts and listens too, but the profound difference between two determining conceptions is set off sharply in the passage which has been our text before: 'The sombre stretch of rounds and hollows seemed to rise and meet the evening gloom in pure sympathy. . . . The place became full of a watchful intentness now; for when other things sank brooding to sleep the heath appeared slowly to awake and listen.' There, compact in two score words, is the very quintessence of Hardy's moors; here, in a sentence, is the very spirit of Meredith's downs, 'fronting the paleness of earliest dawn, and then their arch and curve and dip against the pearly grey of the half-glow; and then, among their hollows, lo, the illumination of the East all around . . . and a gallop for miles along the turfy thymy rolling billows. . . . "It's the nearest hit to wings we can make." ' One of Meredith's characters tells of 'his dream of the winged earth on her flight from splendour to splendour.' That is Meredith's vision too. His beloved Alps hung at dawn beyond the Adriatic, and 'colour . . . wavered in the remoteness, and was quick and dim as though it fell on beating wings,' while beyond 'new heights arose, that soared, or stretched their white uncertain curves in sky like wings traversing infinity.' Even so again, 'wavering in and out of view like flying wings, and shadowed like wings of archangels with rose and with orange and with violet,' the Alps look down on Italy. 'You might take them for mystical streaming torches. . . . They lean as in a great flight forward upon Lombardy.' We have passed from a world above which darkness loves to brood to a world of soaring spaces drenched in light. Even human faces stir in us at times this sense of lifting wings. 'He had a look superior to simple strength and grace; the look of a great sky-bird about to mount'; 'Her face was like the aftersunset across a rose-garden, with the wings of an eagle poised out-spread on the light.' And Sandra Belloni cries: 'My misery now is gladness, is like rain-drops on rising wings.' We are never in Meredith long away from 'the joy of life in steepness overcome And victories of ascent.' France, 'breast-bare, bare-limbed' for conflict is, 'in her bright jet, Earth's crystal spring to sky.' Over against Hardy's in-exorable 'glide of a water-drop down a bud' rise Meredith's mountain-songs, which seem to 'spring like clear water into air, and fall wavering as a feather falls, or the light about a stone in water.' Diana of the Crossways, in the radiance of her young beauty, is 'a spirit leaping and shining like a mountain water.' And as the downs — whose 'long stretching lines are coursing greyhounds in full career' — become to Meredith an image of 'the life in swiftness,' so his winds pervade, like the lifting of wings, his profoundly characteristic figures of spiritual movement upward and ahead. 'Let her life be torn and streaming like the flag of battle, it must be forward to the end.'

> Fruitful sight has Westermain.
> There we laboured, and in turn
> Forward our blown lamps discern.

And finally, in a sentence, the gist of the meaning of men: 'real flesh; a soul born active, *wind-beaten, but ascending.*' And now we reach the heart of Meredith's philosophy.

For that philosophy is essentially terrestrial, not (like Hardy's) cosmic, but it is a philosophy of *ascent*. For earth is more than her beauty; she is flesh of our flesh and bone of our bone, and through us she is spirit too. And in this single aspect of their readings of the riddle, Meredith and Hardy are fundamentally at one. For in each earth somehow comes to consciousness in us. But there the likeness ends. For Hardy's Immanence is a dumb, foresightless dreamer, and we its disordered dream. But the core of earth's meaning to Meredith lies in the fact that 'She [is] Spirit in her clods,' and 'That from flesh unto spirit man grows Even here on the sod under sun.' And again, in the poem

called *Hard Weather*, the wind of Meredith's love
becomes a symbol of 'Life ... at her grindstone set
That she may give us edging keen, String us for
battle.' Because

> [Earth] winnows, winnows roughly; sifts,
> To dip her chosen in her source:
> Contention is the vital force,
> Whence pluck they brain, her prize of gifts,
> *Sky of the senses!* on which height,
> Not disconnected, yet released,
> They see how spirit comes to light.

And spirit, earth-born, is heaven-mounting:

> [Earth's] passion for old giantkind,
> That scaled the mount, uphurled the rock,
> Devolves on them who read aright
> Her meaning and devoutly serve;
> Nor in her starlessness of night
> Peruse her with the craven nerve:
> But even as she from grass to corn,
> To eagle high from grubbing mole,
> Prove in strong brain her noblest born,
> *The station for the flight of soul.*

That, like its noble counterpart with which Goethe's
last recorded conversations end, is tonic doctrine,
and like Hardy's it is self-contained and self-
sufficient. For earth, with her flame of a soul born
of travail of flesh, is her own sole revelation, in
which natural and supernatural are one. And all
this finds, in one of the most profoundly moving
passages in modern poetry, its rich, concrete embodiment in the lovely symbol of the white wild
cherry — that 'young apparition,'

Known, yet wonderful, white
Surpassingly; doubtfully known,
For it struck as the birth of Light:
Even Day from the dark unyoked. . . .
Its beauty to vividness blown,
Drew the life in me forward, chased,
From aloft on a pinnacle's range,
That hindward spidery line,
The length of the ways I had paced,
A footfarer out of the dawn. . . .
She, the white wild cherry, a tree,
Earth-rooted, tangibly wood.
Yet a presence throbbing alive. . . .
> A spirit born of a tree;
> Because earth-rooted alive:
> *Huntress of things worth pursuit*
> *Of souls; in our naming, dreams.*

For dreams, as Meredith conceives them, are Earth's endowment of 'her great venture, Man,' are Earth herself awakening and ascending:

> The dream is an atmosphere;
> A scale still ascending to knit
> The clear to the loftier Clear.
> 'Tis Reason herself, tiptoe
> At the ultimate bound of her wit,
> On the verges of Night and Day.

And in one of the latest poems that vision of Earth ascending spirit-wards through man, which is the heart of Meredith's philosophy, attains exalted utterance:

> Close on the heart of Earth his bosom beats,
> When he the mandate lodged in it obeys,
> Alive to breast a future wrapped in haze,

Strike camp, and onward, like the wind's cloud-fleets.
Unresting she, unresting he, from change
To change, as rain of cloud, as fruit of rain;
She feels her blood-tree throbbing in her grain,
Yet skyward branched, with loftier mark and range.
No miracle the sprout of wheat from clod,
She knows, nor growth of man in grisly brute;
But he, the flower at head and soil at root,
Is miracle, guides he the brute to God.
And that way seems he bound; the way that road,
With his dark-lantern mind, unled, alone,
Wearifully through forest-tracks unsown,
He travels, urged by some internal goad.

And when the long unfolding of that evolution is complete, then (and this is strangely like yet unlike Hardy's final vision)

They shall uplift their Earth to meet her Lord,
Themselves the attuning chord!

And in that great conception of the earnest expectation of a waiting universe, dimly conscious of some vast, far-off, divine event to which the whole creation moves, Meredith and Hardy are at one.

The Poetry of Amy Lowell

The Poetry of Amy Lowell

WE ARE still far too close to the brilliant and arresting personality which was Amy Lowell for a dispassionate appraisal of the one thing for which above all else she cared — her poetry. She was herself, through her vividness and force, the most disturbing factor in our judgment, and no one who knew her can write with entire detachment about her work. One can only speak with sincerity, and trust that one's opinions are not too far from the truth. What, then, accepting once for all these limitations, has she left which has enduring value? All else is after all of secondary moment, and for our purpose we may disregard it here.

When an eager intellectual curiosity is coupled with a spirit of adventure and an indomitable will, things will happen. And when with these qualities there is conjoined a no less eager sense of beauty as revealed in line and light and colour and the potentialities of words and rhythms, the thing that happens will be poetry. And the poetry so engendered will be apt to add to the sum of beauty and to enrich our sense of it in unexpected and sometimes disconcerting ways. And it will also inevitably, in common with all adventuring (and with most things else), fail twice to once that it triumphantly succeeds. Those are the glories — attainment and attempts alike — of the spirit of adventure, and in that inextinguishable spirit the poetry of Amy Lowell is steeped.

I am not sure that this is not indeed its most distinctive characteristic. It flashes like a banner through the pages of *Can Grande's Castle*, and *Legends*, and *Men, Women and Ghosts*. But I suspect that its even more significant expression is found in poems which to all seeming are utterly bare of it. Let me quote one of them which happens to be explicit in its title:

DAWN ADVENTURE

I stood in my window looking at the double cherry:
A great height of white stillness,
Underneath a sky the colour of milky grey jade.
Suddenly a crow flew between me and the tree —
Swooping, falling, in a shadow-black curve —
And blotted himself out in the blurred branches of a leafless ash.
There he stayed for some time, and I could only distinguish
      him by his slight moving.
Then a wind caught the upper branches of the cherry,
And the long, white stems nodded up and down, casually,
      to me in the window.
Nodded — but overhead the grey jade clouds passed slowly,
      indifferently, toward the sea.

— High, white stillness, cut suddenly by a falling curve of black; then a wind in the whiteness, and the friendly signal of the earthborn height, set over against the slow, indifferent movement of the higher height out toward a kindred deep: first a picture, succinct and sparing as a Chinese print; then all at once a touch which opens vistas — in that moment at the window is the sudden thrill of unforeseen experience which is at the heart of all adventure. And the poem is typical of a hundred others. At any moment the familiar may assume one of a thousand fleeting aspects of freshness or surprise. To catch this evanescence, above all to fix it, is perennial adventure and an endless quest. Often enough the swift irradiation is uncaptured, or it dims beneath the intractable medium of words, or in the effort to escape that dulling its intensity is over-wrought. But all that is part of the adventure. And more than any recent poet Amy Lowell sought and missed and won triumphantly experience and expression of those flashes of sudden beauty which pass before most of us can say: 'Lo! there!' — which pass before many of us even know they *are*.

For she has been for years enlarging our boundaries through her own keen, clear perceptions of beauty that most of us have missed, and through her fearlessness in saying precisely what she saw. It was very often not what we saw, and we were apt to question its existence, or at best to dub the thing extreme. It often was; all ardent spirits over-shoot the mark. But when the mark was hit (and that is the sole matter of importance), some familiar, even hackneyed object or experience stood sharply out in fresh and often startling ' beauty. No poet writing today, I think, save Thomas Hardy, saw and heard with more acute perception, or saw and heard and felt so many shades and tones and shapes of things — brilliant and subtle and fugitive and firm. And joined with this quick sensitiveness to physical impressions was an intellectual honesty as sensitive — a passion for truth which never knowingly falsified the report of what was seen. And that alert and vivid sense of beauty, restless with a poet's craving for expression, yet in expression lucidly exact, has schooled us, skeptical and reluctant scholars, to a quickened vision of strange loveliness in familiar things.

I know that to some this emphasis on the familiar will seem capriciously misplaced. But Amy Lowell lived with equal intensity in two worlds. One was the world of the crowded pages of 'The Bronze Horses,' and 'Sea-Blue and Blood-Red,' and 'Guns as Keys; and the Great Gate Swings,' and 'Witch-Woman,' and 'From a Yucca to a Passion-Vine,' and ''Many Swans': the world of the Orient, and of strange legends and superstitions, and of a Past which lay as in a mirror before her, dazzling in its brilliancy and tumultuous with movement — a world as remote as the planet Mars from Brookline Village, Massachusetts. The other was rooted deep in those things which were to her the centre — the things which were *her own*. And the poems which are touched with perhaps the most enduring beauty are those at the heart of which are the objects of her passionate attachment: her garden, the great room in which from sunset till sunrise she lived and talked and wrote, the shifting play of light and colour on trees and birds and sky outside her window, and (merged with all and crowning all) she to whom was dedicated, in *John Keats*, 'This, and all my books.' 'Madonna of the Evening Flowers,' 'Vernal Equinox,' 'Bright Sunlight,' 'July Midnight,' 'The Garden by Moonlight,' 'A Sprig of Rosemary,' 'Penumbra,' 'Prime,' 'Vespers,' 'Summer Night Piece'; 'The Corner of Night and Morning,' 'Beech, Pine, and Sunlight,' 'Planning the Garden,' 'Dog-Days,' 'To Winkey,' 'Lilacs,' 'Purple Grackles' — behind these lies a depth and inwardness unborrowed of the eye:

> A black cat among roses,
> Phlox, lilac-misted under a first-quarter moon,
> The sweet smells of heliotrope and night-scented stock.
> The garden is very still,
> It is dazed with moonlight,
> Contented with perfume,
> Dreaming the opium dreams of its folded poppies.
> Firefly lights open and vanish
> High as the tip buds of the golden glow,
> Low as the sweet alyssum flowers at my feet...
> Only the cat, padding between the roses,
> Shakes a branch and breaks the chequered pattern
> As water is broken by the falling of a leaf.
> Then you come,
> And you are quiet like the garden,
> And white like the alyssum flowers,
> And beautiful as the silent sparks of the fireflies.

> Ah, Beloved, do you see those orange lilies?
> They knew my mother,
> But who belonging to me will they know
> When I am gone?

No one can read that and fail to understand that it was through no happy accident but by virtue of a subtle kinship that the poems of *Fir-Flower Tablets* are, in their exquisite art, among the masterpieces of their kind. They are unique, I suppose, in that their translator knew no Chinese. There is no need to rehearse the story which the book tells for itself of the intimate collaboration with Mrs. Ayscough, who, through her insight into the genius of the language, was to her friend 'the pathway to a new world,' so that the long and arduous task became 'an exciting and inspiring thing.' It was one of the great adventures. And in nothing that Miss Lowell did are the finest qualities of her art more unerringly displayed. Its clarity is no less luminous, but its incised sharpness of line is softened, and its vividness acquires a purer tone. It is as if the mellow serenity of the age-old Orient had descended upon the more restless, keen-edged beauty of a newer world:

> The village is hazy, hazy,
> And mist sucks over the open moor....
> My private rooms are quiet,
> *And calm with the leisure of moonlight through an open door.*

Something of the magic of that tranquil line pervades the volume. And paradoxical as it may seem, more than anywhere else except in her own garden or her own high-walled room, one feels that here Amy Lowell was at home. And one feels, too, that had she lived in the eighth century, by the Peach-Flower Pool and the Swallow Mountains and the Yellow Crane Tower, she would have seen essentially what Li T'ai-po and Tu Fu saw, and would have expressed its breath and finer spirit in a fashion fundamentally the same.

The house of the lonely scholar is in the winding lane.
The great scholar's gate is very high.
The garden pool lies and shines like the magic gall mirror;
Groves of trees throw up flowers with wide, open faces;
The leaf-coloured water draws the Spring sun.
Sitting in the green, covered passage-way, watching the strange,
    red clouds of evening,
Listening to the lovely music of flageolets and strings,
The Golden Valley is not much to boast of.

The clear spring reflects the thin, wide-spreading pine-tree —
And for how many thousand, thousand years?
No one knows.
The late Autumn moon shivers along the little water ripples,
The brilliance of it flows in through the window.
Before it I sit for a long time absent-mindedly chanting,
Thinking of my friend —
What deep thoughts!
There is no way to see him. . . .
   . . . But already the bright hills hold half of the sun between
    their lips. . . .
And, rising, one can see the Autumn moon sliding beneath the
    ripples of the river,
While slowly the sun mounts in the East —
What hope for the revels now?

Precisely what is Amy Lowell and what Li T'ai-po, I neither know nor greatly care. But I do know that she has taken things of beauty which to their readers for centuries were (as they felt them) 'like Spring flowers,' 'like the branches of trees reflected in water — the branches of still trees,' and through her unison with their spirit has recreated their delicate, lingering charm.

I have dwelt on the later lyrics because I believe that among them are the poems which are most surely marked for immortality. But these moments when swift, penetrating vision is subdued to keeping with the mood which it has stirred are but one element in an astonishing profusion. Those of us who have followed the rapid sequence of Miss Lowell's books — or rather, the succession of absorbing interests out of which they sprang — have marvelled at the unabated zest with which fresh fields were entered, searchingly explored, and then annexed. For Amy Lowell had to a high degree the instincts of the scholar bound up, in a nature of singular complexity, with the spirit of adventure and the artist's compelling bent. Sometimes one quality was uppermost, sometimes another; custom never staled her infinite variety. But in the longer, more ambitious poems the student in her, for both good and ill, walked *pari passu* with the adventurer and the poet. In the difficult art of research she was self-taught, but no trained investigator ever brought to his task more tireless energy or a more obstinate determination to find out everything

which for the purpose of the moment could be
learned. That I know, for I have seen it. What it
gave to her poems was a veracity in fundamentals
as remarkable as it is by most of her readers unsus-
pected. For necessarily the artist has transmuted
what the investigator brought. Between what I
have been saying and this declaration of her own
in *Legends* there is not the slightest inconsistency:

> I have changed, added, subtracted, jumbled several
> together at will, left out portions; in short, made them
> over to suit my particular vision.... The truth of
> poetry is imaginative, not literal, and it is as a poet
> that I have conceived and written my book.

So did Chaucer, so did Coleridge, so did Keats.
Read side by side with 'Many Swans' the stark,
primitive Kathlemet legend which so kindled Amy
Lowell's imagination; compare with the 'Legend of
Porcelain' the books on Chinese pottery which gave
to it its lavishness of exquisite detail — do this (to
take no more examples), and there will come fresh
understanding of the ways of the imagination with
its delved and garnered stuff. 'Not that exact
knowledge could help the act of creation,' wrote
Miss Lowell of Keats, 'but that, with knowledge as
a spring-board, imagination could leap with more
certainty of aim.' One could reconstruct Amy
Lowell's ripest *Ars Poetica* from passages scattered
through the pages of *John Keats*, and that last sentence reflects her own experience.

Heaven forbid, however, that I should convey
to anyone (if such there be!) who does not know

Can Grande's Castle or *Legends* the notion that they are academic. They exhaust, on the contrary, one's adjectives (Miss Lowell's were inexhaustible) even to suggest their flashing, impetuous movement, the gaiety and gusto with which their bright, pure, sharply cut images pour along, their combined sweep and concentration, the dramatic contrasts and the stir and tumult of their incidents. I know no writer of English whose command of the rich vocabulary of sensuous impressions approaches Amy Lowell's; the almost physical impact of it startles one each time one turns her pages. But just these qualities which I have mentioned constitute, and always have, a peril to the artist.

There is in Miss Lowell's *Critical Fable* a *tour de force* of self-portraiture — or rather, a gay, sparkling, whimsical portrait of herself as she knew that others saw her. It was not meant to be taken too seriously. But behind its 'gorgeous nonsense' (to use a phrase of Coleridge's) is the humorous detachment of a keen intellect turned with disarming candour upon itself. And one stroke of characterization is particularly apposite here:

> Armed to the teeth like an old Samurai,
> Juggling with jewels like the ancient genii,
> Hung all over with mouse-traps of metres, and cages
> Of bright-plumaged rhythms, with pages and pages
> Of colours slit up into streaming confetti
> Which give the appearance of something sunsetty,
> And gorgeous, and flowing — a curious sight
> She makes in her progress, a modern White Knight,
> Forever explaining her latest inventions. . . .

Nobody who knows the most engaging figure in 'Alice Through the Looking Glass' will miss the half-rueful, half amusedly tolerant point of that. It reminds one irresistibly of an equally candid remark of Coleridge's about his talk:

> The second sort [of talkers] is of those who use five hundred more ideas, images, reasons, etc., than there is any need of to arrive at their object, till the only object arrived at is that the mind's eye of the by-stander is dazzled with colours succeeding so rapidly as to leave one vague impression that there has been a great blaze of colours all about something. Now this is my case, and a grievous fault it is. My illustrations swallow up my thesis.

It was Coleridge, as it happens, who, in 'The Rime of the Ancient Mariner' and 'Christabel' and 'Kubla Khan,' was to Amy Lowell the supreme artist of them all; and both he and she were clear-sighted enough to recognize, the one in his conversation and the other in her verse, the common defect of their quality, which was a too free spending of their affluence — an excess sometimes magnificent, but still excess. And one feels this in Miss Lowell's poetry, I think, precisely where the check of the familiar is withdrawn, and her intensely pictorial imagination revels at will in the exercise of its visualizing energy upon objects and events which (as she says in the Preface to *Can Grande's Castle*) she 'cannot have experienced,' yet which 'seem as actual as [her] own existence.' Of their vivid actuality there can be no question, but we are often dazzled by the unrelieved profusion of brilliant imagery, and instead of the sense of a large simplicity which the Chinese poems leave, we carry away that other impression of the 'great blaze of colours all about something,' which succeeded the most amazing talk of modern times. But that after all is not quite the whole story. I must once more fall back upon Coleridge — who in some mysterious fashion has taken possession of this paragraph! He is speaking of the hero of Miss Lowell's own 'Sea-Blue and Blood-Red': 'To the same enthusiastic sensibilities,' he observes, 'which made a fool of him with regard to his Emma, his country owed the victories of the Nile, Copenhagen, and Trafalgar.' Very well! To the same enthusiastic sensibilities which sometimes overloaded every rift with ore, we owe the thronging impressions which are elsewhere wrought with sovereign restraint into close-girt, straight-sandalled verse.

I am keeping clear of all the theories, whether of Imagism, or cadenced verse, or polyphonic prose. Provocative ideas shot like sparks from an anvil when Amy Lowell talked or wrote, and, being half superb free-lance and half crusader, she delighted in the clash of controversy which she stirred. But I think she had herself ceased to care greatly for what, in effect, were battles long ago. Her past work spoke for itself; there were endless fresh experiences to capture and interpret; and her invincible alacrity of spirit turned to those. The period of dashing swordplay had served its turn. The thing that matters now is the beauty which has emerged serenely from the practice of the theories which once evoked the flashing of so many harmless blades. And this peculiar beauty at its rarest (for perfection is an angel visitant) suggests the clarity of radiant air, and the pure lines of a pattern cut in polished stone — 'clear, reticent, superbly final.'

> For me,
> You stand poised
> In the blue and buoyant air,
> Cinctured by bright winds,
> Treading the sunlight.
> And the waves which precede you
> Ripple and stir
> The sands at my feet.

If those eight lines of 'Venus Transiens' were the only fragment left of an unknown poet, we should recognize that the craftsmanship which wrought their cool, controlled, and shining beauty was unique. And one of the paradoxes of genius is the fact that the most prodigal of poets in her diction could vie, when her art was surest, with the most restrained. Set over against the gorgeous panorama of any section of *Can Grande's Castle* this:

> I might be sighting a tea-clipper,
> Tacking into the blue bay,
> Just back from Canton
> With her hold full of green and blue porcelain,
> And a Chinese coolie leaning over the rail
> Gazing at the white spire
> With dull, sea-spent eyes.

One would not give up either; together they sum
up in little the two ruling impulses, peripheral and
central (to use a critic's phraseology) of a poet who
(to use her own!) 'when not hurricaning's astound-
ingly terse.' She is, at will, precisely that. Every
volume is packed with undetachable examples,
succinct, crisp, often trenchant; bright and brief
(in the words of a poet whom Miss Lowell did not
love!) — bright as 'the flashing of a shield.' But
for renewed assurance one need only turn, in
What's O'Clock, to 'The Anniversary,' and 'Twenty-
Four Hokku on a Modern Theme,' and (for that
matter) 'Evelyn Ray.' Moreover, the exactness
which Miss Lowell loved is nowhere more remarkable than in her sense of the savour and 'feel' of
words:

I want to be a carpenter,
To work all day long in clean wood,
Shaving it into little thin slivers
Which screw up into curls behind my plane;
Pounding square, black nails into white boards,
With the claws of my hammer glistening
Like the tongue of a snake.
I want to shingle a house,
Sitting on the ridge-pole in a bright breeze. . . .
I want to draw a line on a board with a flat pencil,
And then saw along that line,
With the sweet-smelling sawdust piling up in a yellow heap
    at my feet.

Or (as Keats would say), 'Look at flowers — you
know what she says about flowers': blue bells that
are 'Deep tunnels of blue and white dimness, Cool

wine-tunnels for bees'; 'a tide of poppies, Crinkled
and frail and flowing in the breeze'; 'The scent of
hyacinths, like a pale mist' ———

Yes, I know that it will be said again and yet
again that all this is but the beauty of the senses,
'untouched by solemn thought.' I shall not argue
that. Perhaps '[Its] nature is not therefore less
divine.' At all events Miss Lowell found sufficient
answer in a Chinese print:

Red foxgloves against a yellow wall streaked with plum-
    coloured shadows;
A lady with a blue and red sunshade;
The slow dash of waves upon a parapet.
That is all.
Non-existent — immortal —
As solid as the centre of a ring of fine gold.

But in this last book one feels, I think, a deepening of experience, and a beauty less dependent on
the eye. The poignant susceptibility to sense impressions is still there:

> Yet there are sights I see and sounds I hear
> Which ripple me like water as they pass.

There is still the delight in words that are carven
and vivid and luminous as gems; the delight in
rhythms as free yet as poised as the flight of a gull.
And at times there is prodigality in each. But
there has been nothing before in Miss Lowell's
poetry quite like the 'half quizzical, half wistful,'
altogether winning self-revelation in 'The Sisters';
or the mocking lightness of touch and ironic sug-

gestion of 'The Slippers of the Goddess of Beauty';
or the breadth and warmth and (in its true sense)
homeliness of 'Lilacs,' or the sheer lyric intensity of
'Fool o' the Moon.' I am not forgetting 'Meeting-
House Hill'; 'Purple Grackles'; that buoyant skit
on John Keats which bears the title 'View of Teign-
mouth in Devonshire'; the 'Summer Night Piece'
which, like 'Madonna of the Evening Flowers,' is a
dedication; 'Prime' and 'Vespers'; the lines 'To
Carl Sandburg'; the sonnets to Eleanora Duse. But
these bear, some in rare degree, the stamp of a
familiar loveliness. It is the new paths broken that
are significant — now sadly so. For the ripest
years, with disciplined powers and deepening experience behind them and fresh fields before, were
yet to come. *Dis aliter visum.* She has added new
beauty to English poetry. How great that contribu-
tion is will first be clearly seen when time has
winnowed, and her enduring work is brought together in one rare and shining book. It would have
been still richer had she lived. For to the very end
her gallant banner flew. And two lines in this last
volume sum up alike what was and might have
been:

> I ride, ride,
> Seeking those adventures to which I am dedicate.

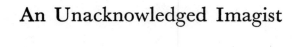

An Unacknowledged Imagist

An Unacknowledged Imagist

Out of the detritus left by bloodless battles long ago the skit which follows has been retrieved, since it touches the subjects of the two essays which immediately precede it. The controversy which prompted it is now as dead as the object — 'so bare, and smooth, and round' — which little Peterkin picked up on the field of the famous victory. It is the excerpts from the prose and verse of George Meredith and Amy Lowell which alone warrant its one day more.

In a letter of gentle remonstrance addressed to the *Little Review* in 1916, Mr. Witter Bynner remarked: 'George Meredith has thousands of imagist poems incidental to each of his novels.' As it happened, I had marked on the fly-leaves of my edition of Meredith some scores of these thousands, but it had not occurred to me to test their *cadences*. Their lucid clarity, their texture 'dur et rare,' their marvellous fidelity to the particular fact, above all (and this is conspicuous by its absence from the Imagist pronouncement) their depth of imaginative insight — all this was obvious enough.

There were images that suggested the clairvoyance of a crystal-gazer, images with the luminous precision of a bit of landscape seen in the reflex of a lens, images that ' "quintessentialized" an emotion until it burnt white-hot,' images crisp, incised, penetrating, 'strait and terse.' But did they fulfil the other requirements of Imagist verse? Did they have 'the quality of *return* . . . the balance which produces the effect of music on the ear'? What follows gives, I think, the answer to that question.

The excerpts entitled 'Winged Regards,' 'Zincali' (1), 'Clair de Lune' (except 4), 'Cedars,' 'What is the colour, etc.,' 'The Pedant,' 'Imagists' (1), 'Aquæ volubiles,' and 'Impavida' are given precisely as they stand, without change or omission of a single word. In 'Our soul is escaped' and 'Zincali' (2), several intervening sentences, in 'Insurgat Aquilo' two intervening paragraphs, are left out. In 'Artemis,' 'Equipoise,' 'Cadences,' 'Sunsets,' 'Beethoven,' a single phrase has been omitted in each case; in 'A Summer Cloud' and 'Imagists' (2), two phrases; in 'Clair de Lune' (4), one word and three cadenced phrases. In 'Gamesters' the excised phrases are more numerous. Barring these omissions, the passages are as Meredith wrote them. It is needless to say that the titles are my own. I have supplied them, not in order to impose an adventitious unity, but to bring out an inherent one.

And first, a number of poems in little — the vignettes, pastels, etchings, cameos, that the Imagists particularly affect. They are, of course, as I am giving them, *bâtons rompus* — a fact, however, which does not detract from their appositeness, for much Imagist verse reads like the culled posies of a florilegium. The impiety of wresting the 'images' which follow from their context would be inexpiable were it not that it serves to throw into sharp relief the fact that, unlike their current counterparts, they *have* a context, are integral parts of a larger whole, and only for the purpose of the moment thus beat their luminous wings in the void.

ARTEMIS

Diana herself,
Gazing at her naked feet;
Her hounds are pricking their ears,
And you see
Antlers of a stag
Behind a block of stone.

WINGED REGARDS

I

He had a look
Superior to simple strength and grace;
The look
Of a great sky-bird
About to mount.

2

Her face
Was like the after-sunset
Across a rose-garden,
With the wings of an eagle
Poised outspread on the light.

EQUIPOISE

Edged moments,
When life is poised
As a crystal pitcher on the head,
In peril of a step.

ZINCALI

I

He was like a Tartar
Modelled by a Greek:
Supple
As the Scythian's bow,
Braced
As the string!

2

Her face
Was like an Egyptian sky
Fronting night.
The strong old Eastern blood
Put ruddy flame
For the red colour.
When she laughed
She illuminated you;
Where she stepped
She made the earth hers.

CADENCES

Mountain songs
That spring
Like clear water into air,
And fall,
Wavering,
As a feather falls,

Or the light
About a stone in water.

CLAIR DE LUNE

1

Over the flowering hawthorn
The moon
Stood like a wind-blown
White rose
Of the heavens.

2

A sleepy fire
Of early moonlight
Hung
Through the dusky fir-branches.

3

A pillar
Of dim silver rain
Fronted the moon
On the hills.

4

The moon
Had now topped the cedar,
And was pure silver.
And in the West,
Facing it,
Was an arch of twilight and tremulous rose;
As if a spirit hung there
Over the shrouded sun.

5

The sky,
Set with very dim distant stars,

Was in grey light
Round a small brilliant moon.
Every space of earth
Lifted clear to her;
The woodland listened;
And in the bright silence
The nightingales sang loud.

SUNSETS

Great red sunsets,
With women kneeling under them.
Do you know those long low sunsets?
They look like blood spilt for love.

CEDARS

1

They saw the cedar
Grey-edged
Under the moon:
And Night,
That clung like a bat
Beneath its ancient open palms.

2

A blue-hued moon
Slipped
From among the clouds,
And hung
In the black outstretched fingers
Of the tree of darkness,
Fronting troubled waters.

BEETHOVEN

I have seen his picture
In shop-windows:

The wind
Seemed in his hair,
And he seemed to hear
With his eyes:
His forehead frowning —
So!

'what is the colour of your eyes and hair?'

Studies for Epipsychidion

I

Smoothed hair
That had the gloss of black briony leaves,
And eyes
Like burning brands
In a cave.

2

Hair
Red as blown flame,
With eyes
Of a grey-green hue,
That may be seen glistening
Over wet sunset.

Her hair
Was radiant in a shady street;
Her eyelids
Tenderly toned
Round the almond enclosure of blue pebbles,
Bright as if shining from the sea wash.

A SUMMER'S CLOUD

They watched it
Lying in the form of a fish,

> Leviathan diminished;
> And the head
> Was lost;
> The tail
> Spread peacockwise —
> And soft to a breath of air
> As gossamer down,
> The body became a ball,
> A cock,
> A little lizard,
> Nothingness.

There are epigrams innumerable. I shall give but three — the last two with due apologies to the saner practitioners of the 'new poetry':

THE PEDANT

> He pores
> Over a little inexactitude
> In phrases,
> And pecks at it
> Like a domestic fowl.

IMAGISTS

1

> Men
> Lying on their backs
> And flying imagination
> Like a kite.

2

> A species
> Of mad metaphor,
> Wriggling and tearing its passage
> Through a thorn-bush,

With the furious urgency
Of a sheep in a panic.

But it is not necessary to be content with min-
iatures. There are flights of stronger wing:

GAMESTERS

A circling white marble ball.
Creatures dabbling over the board
[Like] summer flies on butcher's meat,
Periodically scared by a cloth;
Desperate gleaners,
Hopping,
Skipping,
Bleeding,
Amid a whizz of scythe-blades,
For small wisps
Of booty.

An ancient hoary
Goat-Satan
With skew-eyes and pucker-mouth,
Nursing a hoof
On a knee.
He rolled a ball
For souls,
Excited like kittens,
To catch it.

'OUR SOUL IS ESCAPED . . . '

My heart
Is like a bird
Caught in the hands of a cruel boy.

My misery now
Is gladness,

185

Is like rain-drops
On rising wings,
If I say to myself
'Free! free!'

I fly like a seed
To Italy.
I lift my face to that prospect
As if I smelt new air.

AQUÆ VOLUBILES

See!
The moon is getting whiter.
The water there
Is like a pool of snakes,
And then they struggle out,
And roll over and over,
And stream on lengthwise.
I can see
Their long flat heads,
And their eyes:
Almost their skins.

IMPAVIDA

Lightning
Excited her.
He had seen her lying at her length
Quietly,
Her black hair
Scattered on the pillow,
Like shadow of twigs and sprays
On moonlit grass,
Illuminated intermittently;
Smiling to him,
But her heart out and abroad,
Wild as any witch's.

AN UNACKNOWLEDGED IMAGIST

INSURGAT AQUILO!

A wind was rising.
The trees
Gave their swish of leaves;
The river
Darkened the patch of wrinkles;
The bordering flags amid the reed-blades
Dipped and streamed.

The trees were bending,
The water hissing,
The grasses all this way and that,
Like hands
Of a delirious people
In surges of wreck.[1]

It has been hard to choose. Every lover of Meredith will forthwith double the list. And like the Franklin, 'Lordinges, this question wolde I aske now': Is Meredith writing verse or prose? If prose, what is it that the Imagists are writing?

[1] Since the passages should be susceptible of verification, I append references. The Roman numerals in parenthesis designate chapters. From *The Amazing Marriage*: 'Artemis' (i), 'Winged Regards' 1 (v), 'Equipoise' (xv), 'A Summer's Cloud' (v), 'Gamesters' (ix). From *Sandra Belloni*: 'Winged Regards' 2 (xx), 'Clair de Lune' 1 (xx), 2 (ii), 3 (xii), 4 (xx), 5 (lviii), 'Sunsets' (xx), 'Cedars' 1 (xx), 2 (xxvi), 'Beethoven' (xx), 'What is the colour, etc.,' 1 and 2 (iv), 'Our soul is escaped' (lix), 'Aquæ volubiles' (xx). From *Diana of the Crossways*: 'Zincali' 1 (xiv). From *The Adventures of Harry Richmond*: 'Zincali' 2 (xxiii). From *Vittoria*: 'Cadences' (xxxiii). From *Lord Ormont and his Aminta*: 'What is the colour, etc.,' 3 (xii), 'Impavida' (xxi), 'Insurgat Aquilo' (xxv). From *The Egoist*: 'The Pedant' (xxxiii). From *One of our Conquerors*: 'Imagists' 1 (iv). From *Beauchamp's Career*: 'Imagists' 2 (xii). It will be observed that I have left some of the richest mines untouched.

And now, having printed prose as charming verse, I shall print verse as charming prose. I have chosen three brief excerpts as work of unchallenged beauty and delicate art, which admits the metamorphosis without hint of travesty.[1]

ASTIGMATISM

The Poet took his walking-stick of fine and polished ebony. Set in the close-grained wood were quaint devices; patterns in ambers, and in the clouded green of jades. The top was of smooth, yellow ivory, and a tassel of tarnished gold hung by a faded cord from a hole pierced in the hard wood, circled with silver. For years the Poet had wrought upon this cane. His wealth had gone to enrich it, his experiences to pattern it, his labour to fashion and burnish it. To him it was perfect, a work of art and a weapon, a delight and a defence. The Poet took his walking-stick and walked abroad. . . . The Poet came home at evening, and in the candle-light he wiped and polished his cane. The orange candle flame leaped in the yellow ambers, and made the jades undulate like green pools. It played along the bright ebony, and glowed in the top of cream-coloured ivory. But those things were dead, only the candle-light made them seem to move. 'It is a pity there were no roses,' said the Poet.

MISCAST

I have whetted my brain until it is like a Damascus blade, so keen that it nicks off the floating fringes of passers-by, so sharp that the air would turn its edge were it to be twisted in flight. Licking passions have bitten their arabesques into it, and the mark of them lies, in and out, worm-like, with the beauty of corroded copper patterning white steel. My brain is

---

[1] 'Astigmatism' and 'Miscast' are taken from *Sword Blades and Poppy Seed*; 'Dawn Adventure,' from *Pictures of the Floating World*.

curved like a scimitar, and sighs at its cutting like a sickle mowing grass. But of what use is all this to me! I, who am set to crack stones in a country lane!

DAWN ADVENTURE

I stood in my window looking at the double cherry: a great height of white stillness, underneath a sky the colour of milky grey jade. Suddenly a crow flew between me and the tree — swooping, falling, in a shadow-black curve — and blotted himself out in the blurred branches of a leafless ash. There he stayed for some time, and I could only distinguish him by his slight moving. Then a wind caught the upper branches of the cherry, and the long, white stems nodded up and down, casually, to me in the window, nodded — but overhead the grey jade clouds passed slowly, indifferently, toward the sea.

'Par ma foi,' exclaimed M. Jourdain, with the light of a great discovery in his eyes — 'par ma foi, il y a plus de quarante ans que je dis de la prose sans que j'en susse rien.' I have no desire to press the point. One may be well content to accept beauty where and in whatever garb one finds it, and leave the academic appraisals of the moment to the impartial winnowing of time.